G.E. Syme T.W. Ireland

# PRENTICE-HALL ACCOUNTING

## Student Workbook

## B

(Chapters 13 – 18
and Supplementary Exercise)



Prentice-Hall Canada Inc.

**Canadian Cataloguing in Publication Data**

Syme, G. E.
Prentice-Hall accounting. Student workbook B
(chapters 13–18)

Supplement to: Syme, G. E. Prentice-Hall accounting.
Ch. 13–18.
ISBN 0-13-715749-5

1. Accounting — Problems, exercises, etc.
I. Ireland, T. W. II. Title.

HF5635.S923 1990 657'.042 C89-090696-3

*Also available:*
**Student Text** 0-13-715939-0
**Teacher's Guide** 0-13-715756-8 (includes Computer Files disks)
**Supplementary Material:** Teacher's Key A (Chapters 1–12) 0-13-715715-0
Teacher's Key B (Chapters 13–18) 0-13-715723-1
Student Workbook A (Chapters 1–12) 0-13-715731-2



PRENTICE-HALL INC., Englewood Cliffs, New Jersey
PRENTICE-HALL INTERNATIONAL, INC., London
PRENTICE-HALL OF AUSTRALIA, PTY., LTD., Sydney
PRENTICE-HALL OF INDIA, PVT., LTD., New Delhi
PRENTICE-HALL OF JAPAN, INC., Tokyo
PRENTICE-HALL OF SOUTHEAST ASIA (PTE.), LTD., Singapore
EDITORA PRENTICE-HALL DO BRASIL, LTDA., Rio de Janeiro
PRENTICE-HALL HISPANOAMERICANA, S.A., Mexico

ISBN 0-13-715749-5

Project Editors: Julia Lee, Denyse O'Leary
Production Editor: Pam Young
Production Co-ordinator: Crystale Chalmers
Typesetting: Siegfried Betterman Communications

5 6 7 WC 03 02 01

Printed and bound in Canada by Webcom Limited

# Contents

# Preface

*Prentice-Hall Accounting Student Workbooks A* and *B* supply all the business papers and accounting forms required to complete the exercises in the student text. *Teacher's Key A (Chapters 1–12)* and *B (Chapters 13–18)* are an exact replica of the Workbooks, with the answers to all textbook and Workbook questions and exercises keyed in.

Many teachers find it useful to be able to show the correct answers to their students. For this reason, we are giving users of the *Prentice-Hall Accounting* text permission to reproduce any or all of the pages in the Teacher's Keys. You may wish to make overheads, handouts, or displays for your bulletin board. However you wish to do it, we hope you will use this material to the full.

*Teacher's Keys A and B* supplement the Workbooks. These manuals are designed to assist teachers by supplying worked-out solutions for all exercises, answers for all review questions, and comments on the case studies. *Teacher's Key A* answers questions in Chapters 1 through 12 and the Summary Exercise; *Teacher's Key B* answers questions in Chapters 13 through 18, including the Supplementary Exercise. Computer exercises requiring actual programming are not dealt with in the *Teacher's Keys*, but in the *Prentice-Hall Accounting* Computer Files and in the *Teacher's Guide*.

Finally, a *Teacher's Guide* is available for the program. For each chapter of the student text, this guide offers:

- an overview of the chapter;
- a chapter schedule, indicating the approximate time each section should take to teach;
- comments for each section within the chapter, including suggestions for the introduction of a topic, ideas on how to extend a particular concept, and comments on section exercises, as well as notes about extra materials required (e.g., black-line masters, an overhead projector, supplementary books);
- comments on end-of-chapter exercises;
- comments on the careers and entrepreneur opportunities;
- black-line masters to illustrate the major concepts covered in the chapter;
- two tests, including comprehension questions as well as exercises. Selected chapters also have computer knowledge quizzes. (There are no tests for Chapter 1.)
- an appendix on teaching about computers in accounting;
- disks containing the masters for the hands-on computer exercises.

G.E.S. T.W.I.

# Chapter 13 Cash Control and Banking

## ANSWERS TO SECTION 13.1 REVIEW QUESTIONS (text, p. 474)

### Personal Banking

1. ______________________

2. ______________________

3. ______________________
4. ______________________
5. ______________________
6. ______________________
7. ______________________
8. ______________________
9. ______________________

10. ______________________
11. ______________________
12. ______________________

13. ______________________

14. ______________________

15. ______________________
16. ______________________

## ANSWERS TO SECTION 13.1 EXERCISES (text, p. 475)

### Exercise 1, p. 475

1. Banks provide ______________ for both individuals and businesses.
2. One of the essential services provided by banks is the ____________ of money.
3. Another of the essential services provided by banks is the ________ of money.
4. Of the three most common types of personal bank accounts, the __________________ gives the highest rate of interest.

 Name____________________ Date________________

## ANSWERS TO SECTION 13.1 EXERCISES (cont.)

**Ex. 1 (cont.)**

5. A bank statement is provided each month with the _________________________.
6. A ___________ record of a savings account is provided.
7. It is advisable for the individual to keep a _____________________.
8. The ________________________ is the simplest form of personal bank record.
9. A cheque that the bank will not cash because of insufficient funds is known as an _______________.
10. A ___________________ is one for which the bank takes the funds out of the account in advance.
11. A certified cheque will not _________.
12. A ______________________ is one that is dated for some time in the future.
13. The usual reason for writing post-dated cheques is in respect to a ______________________ such as for a mortgage.

**Exercise 2, p. 475**

Indicate whether each of the following statements is true or false by placing a "T" or an "F" in the space indicated. Explain the reason for each "F" response in the space provided below.

1. A pure savings account is designed for the person who leaves money in the account relatively untouched. ☐
2. You are not allowed to write cheques on a pure savings account. Therefore, you can only get money out of a pure savings account by closing out the account. ☐
3. The interest rate on a daily interest savings account is always about one-half a point higher than it is on a pure savings account. ☐
4. A passbook record of a savings account can only be updated at the bank. ☐
5. The personal chequing account is not intended to be used for saving money. ☐
6. There is no limit to the number of cheques that can be written on a personal chequing account. ☐
7. A personal bank record is not really necessary because the bank keeps a record of your account. ☐
8. If Joan Arnott's bank balance as shown by the bank is $352, she can write a cheque for that much money with no fear of its bouncing. ☐
9. A cheque is considered to be cash, but it is not assured cash until it has been cleared by the banking system. ☐
10. The purpose of endorsing a cheque is so the bank can compare the endorsement with the signature card. ☐
11. When you deposit a cheque the bank gives you immediate credit for the amount even though the cheque might bounce. ☐
12. You visit your sister-in-law's bank to cash a cheque for $100 that she has given to you. The bank informs you that there is only $90 in your sister-in-law's account and gives you the $90. ☐

## Chapter 13

Name ____________________ Date ____________

### ANSWERS TO SECTION 13.1 EXERCISES (cont.)

**Ex. 2 (cont.)**

**13.** You should request cash or a certified cheque when you sell a used car to a stranger. ☐

**14.** On March 15, 19 – 1, the bank will refuse to cash a cheque dated March 20, 19 – 1. ☐

**Explanations**

______________________________________________

______________________________________________

______________________________________________

______________________________________________

______________________________________________

______________________________________________

**Exercise 3, p. 476**

### GENERAL JOURNAL

PAGE ________

| DATE | | PARTICULARS | P.R. | DEBIT | CREDIT |
|---|---|---|---|---|---|
| *1.* | | | | | |
| | | | | | |
| | | | | | |
| | | | | | |
| | | | | | |
| *2.* | | | | | |
| | | | | | |
| | | | | | |

## ANSWERS TO SECTION 13.1 EXERCISES (cont.)

### Exercise 4, p. 476

GENERAL JOURNAL PAGE ________

| DATE | | PARTICULARS | P.R. | DEBIT | CREDIT |
|---|---|---|---|---|---|
| 1. | | | | | |
| | | | | | |
| | | | | | |
| | | | | | |
| | | | | | |
| 2. | | | | | |
| | | | | | |
| | | | | | |
| | | | | | |
| 3. | | | | | |
| | | | | | |
| | | | | | |

## ANSWERS TO SECTION 13.2 REVIEW QUESTIONS (text, p. 479)

### Bank Credit Cards

1. ____________________
2. ____________________
3. ____________________
4. ____________________

## ANSWERS TO SECTION 13.2 EXERCISES (text, p. 479)

### Exercise 1, p. 479

1. Today's society is often referred to as a ________ society.
2. Credit cards sponsored by the chartered banks are ____________ and ____.
3. Bank credit cards can be used in most ____________.

 Name________________________ Date__________________

## ANSWERS TO SECTION 13.2 EXERCISES (cont.)

**Ex. 1 (cont.)**

4. During or at the end of the day the credit card slips are prepared for inclusion in the ____________ ________.
5. The merchant does not get full value for the ____________ of the credit card slips.
6. Each month the bank charges the merchant with a ____________.

**Exercise 2, p. 480**

Indicate whether each of the following statements is true or false by placing a "T" or an "F" in the space indicated. Explain each "F" response in the space provided below.

1. Small retail outlets do not offer their own individualized credit cards because they prefer not sell on credit. ☐
2. Carrying a bank credit card is like having plastic money. ☐
3. The use of credit cards slows things down at the cash register. ☐
4. During, or at the end of the day, the bank credit card slips are included in the bank deposit. ☐
5. The two common bank credit cards are Visa and Mastercard. ☐
6. Bank credit cards services would probably not have become widely available without the development of the computer. ☐
7. The merchant never has to worry about collecting his money if a customer offers a credit card in payment. ☐
8. When accounting for the day's bank credit card sales, the debit is to Accounts Receivable (credit card centre). ☐

**Explanations**

________________________________________________________________

________________________________________________________________

________________________________________________________________

________________________________________________________________

________________________________________________________________

 Name______________________ Date______________

## ANSWERS TO SECTION 13.2 EXERCISES (cont.)

### Exercise 3, p. 480

1. 
2. 
3. 
4. 
5. 
6. 
7. 
8. 
9. 
10. 

### Exercise 4, p. 481

1. 
2. 
3. 
4. 
5. 
6. 
7. 
8. 
9. 
10. 
11. 

# Chapter 13

Name ______________________ Date ______________

## ANSWERS TO SECTION 13.3 REVIEW QUESTIONS (text, p. 491)

### Banking for a Business

1. ______________________

2. ______________________

3. ______________________

4. ______________________

5. ______________________

6. ______________________

7. ______________________

8. ______________________

9. ______________________

10. ______________________

11. ______________________

12. ______________________

13. ______________________

14. ______________________

15. ______________________

16. ______________________

17. ______________________

18. ______________________

19. ______________________

# Chapter 13

Name______________________ Date______________

## ANSWERS TO SECTION 13.3 EXERCISES (text, p. 493)

**Exercise 1, p. 493**

1. The ____________ of a business represent the money taken in from business operations.
2. It is customary for a business that ____________ to receive payment from its customers by way of cheques through the mail.
3. Cheques received in the mail are _____ by the mail clerk before being deposited in the bank.
4. Sales slips are ____________ to ensure that all slips are accounted for.
5. In a business where goods are sold for cash, the cash is ________ at the end of the day.
6. An electronic cash register that is connected to a central computer is known as a ____________ ________.
7. A small quantity of money used to start the cash register activity for the day is known as a ______ ___.
8. Cash registers can be used for transactions other than just __________.
9. As transactions occur during the day, the details are stored inside the cash register on a paper tape known as the ________ or the ______________.
10. At the end of each day the daily balance form, the cash, and the vouchers are forwarded to the ______________________.
11. Cash ________ are more common than cash ________.
12. Businesses are required by the banks to use a __________________.
13. All cheques received by the business are endorsed ______________ before being deposited.
14. Business deposit slips are prepared in ________.
15. When preparing the cash for deposit, bills are sorted by ____________.

## ANSWERS TO SECTION 13.3 EXERCISES (cont.)

**Exercise 2, p. 494**

1. **SUMMARY SHEET**

SALES SUMMARY — DATE *November 15* 19 —

SIGNATURE *S*

| | SALES | SALES TAX | TOTAL |
|---|---|---|---|
| CHARGE SALES SLIPS | | | |
| LESS CREDITS | | | |
| NET CHARGE SALES SLIPS | | | |
| CASH SALES SLIPS | | | |
| LESS REFUNDS | | | |
| NET CASH SALES SLIPS | | | |
| RECEIPTS ON ACCOUNT | | | |
| TOTAL CASH PER SLIPS | | | |
| ACTUAL CASH ON HAND | | | |
| CASH SHORT ___ OR OVER ___ | | | |
| TOTALS | | | |

**ACCOUNTING ENTRY**

2.

| Accounts | Dr | Cr |
|---|---|---|
| | | |
| | | |
| | | |
| | | |
| | | |
| | | |
| | | |

 Name________ Date________

## ANSWERS TO SECTION 13.3 EXERCISES (cont.)

**Exercise 3, p. 494**

CASH PROOF AND ACCOUNTING SUMMARY

DATE *February 28*, 19—

| | TO LINE NO. | TOTALS | | |
|---|---|---|---|---|
| **CASH REGISTER TOTALS** | | | | |
| Cash Sales less Refunds (Incl. Tax) | — | 1 | 325 | 73 |
| Visa Sales less Visa Returns (Incl. Tax) | 2 | | 843 | 16 |
| Charge Sales (Incl. Tax) | 3 | | 525 | 37 |
| Received on Account | 8 | | 295 | |
| Returns for Credit (Incl. Tax) | 9 | | 87 | 74 |
| Paid Outs | — | | 40 | 00 |
| Sales Less Returns | 10 | 2 | 436 | 00 |
| Sales Tax (Net) | 11 | | 170 | 52 |
| **CASH PROOF** | | | | |
| Total Cash Received Less Paid Outs | — | 1 | 580 | 73 |
| Cash by Actual Count | 1 | | | |
| Cash Short | 7 | | | |
| Cash Over | 12 | | | |
| **PAID OUTS BREAKDOWN** | | | | |
| Account______ | 4 | | | |
| Account______ | 5 | | | |
| Account______ | 6 | | | |
| Total Paid Outs | | | 40 | – |

ACCOUNTING ENTRY

| LINE NO. | ACCOUNTS | | DR | CR |
|---|---|---|---|---|
| 1 | Cash | Total to Bank | | |
| 2 | Visa | | | |
| 3 | Accounts Rec'l (Charge Sales) | | | |
| 4 | Asset or Expense______ | | | |
| 5 | Asset or Expense______ | | | |
| 6 | Asset or Expense______ | | | |
| 7 | Cash Short or Over | | | |
| 8 | Accounts Rec'l (Rec'd on A/c) | | | |
| 9 | Accounts Rec'l (Ret'd for Cr.) | | | |
| 10 | Sales | | | |
| 11 | Sales Tax Payable | | | |
| 12 | Cash Short or Over | | | |
| | BALANCING TOTALS | | | |

CASHIER'S SIGNATURE

## ANSWERS TO SECTION 13.3 EXERCISES (cont.)

**Ex. 3 (cont.)**

| Summary of Vouchers | | | | | | | | | | | | | | |
|---|---|---|---|---|---|---|---|---|---|---|---|---|---|---|
| Charge Sales | | | Visa Sales | | | Received on Acct. | | | Paid Outs | | | Credit Notes | | |
| | | | | | | | | | | | | | | |

**Exercise 4, p. 495 (Workbook Exercise)**

**Using the information shown below, perform the following:**

1. On the daily balance form provided, fill in the totals that would be machine printed by the cash register on May 5, 19 —.
2. Complete the remainder of the form.
3. Show that the vouchers agree with the appropriate summary figures.

**Additional Information**

a. *Cash Register Daily Totals*

| | | | |
|---|---|---|---|
| $1 755.87 | CASL | 262.15 | CRDT |
| 2 635.41 | VISA | 320.95 | TAX |
| 1 470.00 | RECD | 4 585.00 | MDS |
| 75.50 | P.O. | 3 150.37 | CASH |
| 776.82 | CHRG | | |

b. *Cash on Hand, Including $50 float*

| | | | |
|---|---|---|---|
| Bills | $20 × 85 | Coin | 1¢ × 210 |
| | $10 × 83 | | 5¢ × 240 |
| | $ 5 × 54 | | 10¢ × 190 |
| | $ 2 × 42 | | |
| | $ 1 × 117 | | 25¢ × 713 |

c. *Vouchers on Hand*

Sales slip No. 29, Visa sale for 277.13.
Sales slip No. 30, credit note for $112.35.
Sales slip No. 31, Visa sale for $437.63.
Sales slip No. 32, received on account, $500.
Sales slip No. 33, Visa sale for $426.93.
Sales slip No. 34, Visa sale for $197.95.
Sales slip No. 35, received on account, $350.
Sales slip No. 36, charge sale for $347.75.
Supplier's bill, for supplies, $35.52.
Sales slip No. 37, charge sale for $429.07.
Sales slip No. 38, credit note for $149.80.
Sales slip No. 39, received on account, $250.
Sales slip No. 40, Visa sale for $215.07.
Supplier's bill, for Miscellaneous Expense, $39.98
Sales slip No. 41, Visa sale for $535.00.
Sales slip No. 42, Visa sale for $545.70.
Sales slip No. 43, received on account, $370.00.

 Name________________________ Date__________

## ANSWERS TO SECTION 13.3 EXERCISES (cont.)

**Ex. 4 (cont.)**

CASH PROOF AND ACCOUNTING SUMMARY

DATE *May 5*, 19—

| | TO LINE NO. | TOTALS | | |
|---|---|---|---|---|
| **CASH REGISTER TOTALS** | | | | |
| Cash Sales less Refunds (Incl. Tax) | — | 1 | 755 | 87 |
| Visa Sales less Visa Returns (Incl. Tax) | 2 | 2 | 635 | 41 |
| Charge Sales (Incl. Tax) | 3 | | 776 | 82 |
| Received on Account | 8 | 1 | 470 | 00 |
| Returns for Credit (Incl. Tax) | 9 | | 262 | 15 |
| Paid Outs | — | | 75 | 50 |
| Sales Less Returns | 10 | 4 | 585 | 00 |
| Sales Tax (Net) | 11 | | 320 | 95 |
| **CASH PROOF** | | | | |
| Total Cash Received Less Paid Outs | — | 3 | 150 | 37 |
| Cash by Actual Count | 1 | | | |
| Cash Short | 7 | | | |
| Cash Over | 12 | | | |
| **PAID OUTS BREAKDOWN** | | | | |
| Account________ | 4 | | | |
| Account________ | 5 | | | |
| Account________ | 6 | | | |
| Total Paid Outs | | | 75 | 50 |

ACCOUNTING ENTRY

| LINE NO. | ACCOUNTS | DR | CR |
|---|---|---|---|
| 1 | Cash | | |
| 2 | Visa — Total to Bank | | |
| 3 | Accounts Rec'l (Charge Sales) | | |
| 4 | Asset or Expense________ | | |
| 5 | Asset or Expense________ | | |
| 6 | Asset or Expense________ | | |
| 7 | Cash Short or Over | | |
| 8 | Accounts Rec'l (Rec'd on A/c) | | |
| 9 | Accounts Rec'l (Ret'd for Cr.) | | |
| 10 | Sales | | |
| 11 | Sales Tax Payable | | |
| 12 | Cash Short or Over | | |
| | BALANCING TOTALS | | |

CASHIER'S SIGNATURE

## ANSWERS TO SECTION 13.3 EXERCISES (cont.)

**Ex. 4 (cont.)**

| Summary of Vouchers | | | | | | | | | | | | | |
|---|---|---|---|---|---|---|---|---|---|---|---|---|---|
| Charge Sales | | | Visa Sales | | | Received on Acct. | | | Credit Notes | | | Paid Outs | |
| | | | | | | | | | | | | | |

**Exercise 5, p. 495**

| |
|---|
| *1.* |
| *2.* |
| *3.* |
| *4.* |

## ANSWERS TO SECTION 13.3 EXCERCISES (cont.)

**Exercise 6, p. 496**

**1., 2.**

**cheques**

| CREDIT ACCOUNT NO. | DATE |
|---|---|
| NAME | |
| | |

| PARTICULARS | AMOUNT | |
|---|---|---|
| | | |
| | | |
| | | |
| | | |
| | | |
| | | |
| | | |
| | | |
| | | |
| | | |
| | | |
| | | |
| | | |
| | | |
| TOTAL CHEQUES (CARRY FORWARD) | | |

* 

**CURRENT ACCOUNT DEPOSIT**

**Commercial Bank**

| CREDIT ACCOUNT NO. | DATE |
|---|---|
| NAME | |
| | |
| DEPOSITED BY | |

| | | |
|---|---|---|
| × 1 | | |
| × 2 | | |
| × 5 | | |
| × 10 | | |
| × 20 | | |
| × 50 | | |
| × 100 | | |
| | | |
| COIN | | |
| SUB-TOTAL / TELLER | | |
| VISA | | |
| U.S. CHEQUES | | |
| U.S. CASH | | |
| * TOTAL CHEQUES (BROUGHT FORWARD) | | |
| | | |
| U.S CHEQUES (PLUS/MINUS) | | |
| * GRAND TOTAL > | | |

**CURRENT ACCOUNT DEPOSIT**

## ANSWERS TO SECTION 13.4 REVIEW QUESTIONS (text, p. 502)

### Accounting Controls for Cash

1. ______________________________

2. ______________________________
3. ______________________________
4. ______________________________

5. ______________________________

6. ______________________________

7. ______________________________
8. ______________________________

9. ______________________________

10. ______________________________

11. ______________________________

12. ______________________________

13. ______________________________

14. ______________________________

## ANSWERS TO SECTION 13.4 EXERCISES (text, p. 502)

**Exercise 1, p. 502**

1. ______________________________

2. ______________________________

 Name________________ Date__________

## ANSWERS TO SECTION 13.4 EXERCISES (cont.)

**Ex. 1 (cont.)**

**3.** ______________________________

**4.** ______________________________

**5.** ______________________________

**6.** ______________________________

**7.** ______________________________

**8.** ______________________________

**9.** ______________________________

**10.** ______________________________

**11.** ______________________________

**12.** ______________________________

## ANSWERS TO SECTION 13.4 EXERCISES (cont.)

**Exercise 2, p. 504**

**1.**

*Paul Swartz*
*Bank Reconciliation*
*June 30, 19 —*

| *Personal Record* | | *Bank Statement* | |
|---|---|---|---|
| | | | |
| | | | |
| | | | |
| | | | |
| | | | |
| | | | |

**2.** ________________________________________

________________________________________

________________________________________

**Exercise 3, p. 506 (Workbook Exercise)**

The information given below includes the personal chequing account record and the bank statement for the account of Joy Lopez for the month of June. Joy Lopez's bank reconciliation for May is also included.

1. From these records, reconcile the bank account as of June 30.
2. List the entries or corrections necessary in the personal record of Joy Lopez to bring the balance to the true figure.

**a. Previous reconciliation.**

*Joy Lopez*
*Bank Reconciliation*
*May 31, 19 —*

| *Personal Record* | | *Bank Statement* | | |
|---|---|---|---|---|
| *Latest Balance* | 519 95 | *Latest Balance* | | 424 40 |
| *Deduct: Bank Service Charge* | 5 00 | *Add: Late Deposit* | | 297 00 |
| *True Bank Balance* | 514 95 | | | 721 40 |
| | | *Deduct: Outstanding cheques* | | |
| | | #137 | 45 00 | |
| | | #138 | 37 50 | |
| | | #139 | 123 95 | 206 45 |
| | | *True Bank Balance* | | 514 95 |

## ANSWERS TO SECTION 13.4 EXERCISES (cont.)

**Ex. 3 (cont.)**

**b. Joy Lopez's personal record.**

| CHEQUE NO. | DATE 19— | CHEQUE ISSUED TO | AMOUNT OF CHEQUE | | ✔ | AMOUNT OF DEPOSIT | | BALANCE FORWARD | |
|---|---|---|---|---|---|---|---|---|---|
| | | | | | | | | 681 | 40 |
| 138 | May 29 | Fred's Foods | 37 | 50 | | | | 643 | 90 |
| 139 | 31 | Mountain Fuels | 123 | 95 | | | | 519 | 95 |
| | Jun 1 | Service Charge | 5 | – | | | | 514 | 95 |
| 140 | 2 | Telephone | 26 | 75 | | | | 488 | 75 |
| 141 | 5 | Hydro | 47 | 30 | | | | 441 | 45 |
| 142 | 9 | Property Tax | 273 | – | | | | 168 | 45 |
| 144 | 11 | Bay Store | 65 | 19 | | | | 103 | 26 |
| | 12 | Paycheque less $100 | | | | 850 | – | 953 | 26 |
| 145 | 17 | Ski Club | 33 | – | | | | 920 | 26 |
| 146 | 19 | Dr. McGail | 30 | – | | | | 890 | 26 |
| 147 | 22 | Undercover | 14 | 98 | | | | 875 | 28 |
| 148 | 24 | Eaton's | 6 | 90 | | | | 868 | 38 |
| | 26 | Paycheque less $100 | | | | 800 | – | 1 668 | 38 |
| 149 | 29 | Western Sails | 410 | – | | | | 1 258 | 38 |
| 150 | 30 | Frank Topa | 335 | – | | | | 923 | 38 |
| 151 | 30 | Pete's Sports | 46 | 20 | | | | 877 | 18 |
| 152 | 30 | Cash Withdrawal | 150 | – | | | | 727 | 18 |
| | 30 | Insurance Refund | | | | 135 | – | 862 | 18 |
| | | | | | | | | | |
| | | | | | | | | | |

## ANSWERS TO SECTION 13.4 EXERCISES (cont.)

**Ex. 3 (cont.)**

**c. Bank statement sent to Joy Lopez.**

**Municipal Bank**

STATEMENT OF ACCOUNT FOR Joy Lopez

| CHEQUES | | DEPOSITS | DATE | BALANCE |
|---|---|---|---|---|
| Balance forward | | | May 31 | 424.40 |
| | | 297.00 | June 1 | 721.40 |
| 45.00 | | | June 2 | 676.40 |
| 123.95 | | | June 4 | 552.45 |
| 26.75 | | | June 5 | 525.70 |
| 37.50 | | | June 9 | 488.20 |
| 150.00 | (withdrawal) | | June 10 | 338.20 |
| | | 850.00 | June 12 | 1 188.20 |
| 273.00 | | | June 15 | 915.20 |
| 47.30 | 65.19 | | June 16 | 802.71 |
| 30.00 | | | June 23 | 772.71 |
| 14.98 | | | June 24 | 757.73 |
| | | 800.00 | June 26 | 1 557.73 |
| 6.90 | | | June 30 | 1 550.83 |
| 150.00 | (withdrawal) | | June 30 | 1 398.63 |
| S.C. 2.20 | | | | |

S.C. Service Charge

## ANSWERS TO SECTION 13.4 EXERCISES (cont.)

**Ex. 3 (cont.)**

1.

Joy Lopez

Bank Reconciliation

June 30, 19—

| Personal Record | | Bank Statement | |
|---|---|---|---|
| | | | |
| | | | |
| | | | |
| | | | |
| | | | |
| | | | |
| | | | |
| | | | |
| | | | |

2.

**Exercise 4, p. 506**

1. ____________
2. ____________
3. ____________
4. ____________
5. ____________
6. ____________

 Name____________________ Date____________

## ANSWERS TO SECTION 13.5 REVIEW QUESTIONS (text, p. 510)

### Petty Cash Fund

1. ____________________
2. ____________________
3. ____________________
4. ____________________
5. ____________________
6. ____________________
7. ____________________
8. ____________________
9. ____________________
10. ____________________

## ANSWERS TO SECTION 13.5 EXERCISES (text, p. 510)

**Exercise 1, p. 510**

GENERAL JOURNAL PAGE ________

| DATE 19— | PARTICULARS | P.R. | DEBIT | CREDIT |
|---|---|---|---|---|
| | | | | |
| | | | | |
| | | | | |
| | | | | |
| | | | | |

## ANSWERS TO SECTION 13.5 EXERCISES (cont.)

**Exercise 2, p. 510**

**GENERAL JOURNAL** PAGE ______

| DATE | | PARTICULARS | P.R. | DEBIT | CREDIT |
|---|---|---|---|---|---|
| | | | | | |
| | | | | | |
| | | | | | |
| | | | | | |
| | | | | | |

**Exercise 3, p. 510**

| | | | | | |
|---|---|---|---|---|---|
| | | | | | |
| | | | | | |
| | | | | | |
| | | | | | |
| | | | | | |
| | | | | | |
| | | | | | |
| | | | | | |
| | | | | | |
| | | | | | |
| | | | | | |
| | | | | | |
| | | | | | |
| | | | | | |
| | | | | | |

## ANSWERS TO SECTION 13.5 EXERCISES (cont.)

**Ex. 3 (cont.)**

GENERAL JOURNAL PAGE ______

| DATE | | PARTICULARS | P.R. | DEBIT | CREDIT |
|---|---|---|---|---|---|
| | | | | | |
| | | | | | |
| | | | | | |
| | | | | | |
| | | | | | |
| | | | | | |
| | | | | | |
| | | | | | |
| | | | | | |
| | | | | | |
| | | | | | |

**Exercise 4, p. 511**

1.

| | | | | | |
|---|---|---|---|---|---|
| | | | | | |
| | | | | | |
| | | | | | |
| | | | | | |
| | | | | | |
| | | | | | |
| | | | | | |
| | | | | | |
| | | | | | |
| | | | | | |
| | | | | | |
| | | | | | |
| | | | | | |
| | | | | | |
| | | | | | |
| | | | | | |
| | | | | | |
| | | | | | |
| | | | | | |

## ANSWERS TO SECTION 13.5 EXERCISES (cont.)

**Ex. 4 (cont.)**

**2.** **GENERAL JOURNAL** PAGE ______

| DATE | | PARTICULARS | P.R. | DEBIT | CREDIT |
|---|---|---|---|---|---|
| | | | | | |
| | | | | | |
| | | | | | |
| | | | | | |
| | | | | | |
| | | | | | |
| | | | | | |
| | | | | | |

**Exercise 5, p. 511**

Indicate whether each of the following statements is true or false by placing a "T" or an "F" in the space indicated. Explain the reason for each "F" response in the space provided below.

1. The Petty Cash account in the general ledger must never change. ☐
2. A Petty Cash voucher must be prepared for every payment out of the fund. ☐
3. The petty cash fund is used for the purpose of cutting down on the number of cheques used. ☐
4. The accounting entry to replenish the petty cash fund is made by the keeper of the fund. ☐
5. The petty cash box is locked and put away in a safe place outside business hours. ☐
6. The keeper of the petty cash fund must never borrow from it. ☐
7. The petty cash summary is organized by general ledger accounts. ☐
8. A payment out of petty cash can only be charged to an expense account or an asset account. ☐
9. The keeper of the fund is expected to make up any shortage in the petty cash fund. ☐

# Chapter 13

Name ______________________ Date ____________

## ANSWERS TO SECTION 13.5 EXERCISES (cont.)

**Ex. 5 (cont.)**

**10.** If the auditor were to check the petty cash fund, the procedure would be to total all of the cash and vouchers in the box and to check this total against the balance in the Petty Cash account. ☐

**Explanations**

______________________________________________

______________________________________________

______________________________________________

______________________________________________

______________________________________________

______________________________________________

## ANSWERS TO SECTION 13.6 REVIEW QUESTIONS (text, p. 513)

### Accounting Controls for Expenditures

1. ______________________________________________

   ______________________________________________
2. ______________________________________________
3. ______________________________________________
4. ______________________________________________
5. ______________________________________________
6. ______________________________________________

## ANSWERS TO SECTION 13.6 EXERCISES (text, p. 513)

**Exercise 1, p. 513**

1. Poor accounting controls can result in the payment of bills that were ____________ sent to the business.
2. The voucher system is a method of processing ______________________.
3. The ______________ is effective because it controls expenditures through a rigid set of verification procedures.
4. Any document used in the voucher system as part of the verification process is a ________.
5. The purchasing department formally orders goods when it issues a ______________.
6. A ______________ contains detailed information about goods received from suppliers.
7. The ______________ is a combination file folder and voucher approval form.

## ANSWERS TO SECTION 13.6 EXERCISES (cont.)

### Exercise 2, p. 516

1. ______________________________
2. ______________________________
3. ______________________________
4. ______________________________
5. ______________________________
6. ______________________________
7. ______________________________
8. ______________________________
9. ______________________________
10. ______________________________
11. ______________________________
12. ______________________________

### Exercise 3, p. 516

1.

# Voucher Approval Form

Supplier ____________________ Voucher No. __________

Address ____________________

____________________

____________________

Invoice Date ____________________

Invoice Amount ____________________

Discount ____________________

Net Amount ____________________

Payment Date ____________________

| | |
|---|---|
| Purchase Order Checked | |
| Description | |
| Price | |
| Terms | |
| Goods or Services Rec'd | |
| Calculations Checked | |
| Accounting Distribution | |
| Approved for Payment | |

2. ACCOUNTING DISTRIBUTION

| | | | | |
|---|---|---|---|---|
| Debits: | Purchases | | | |
| | Supplies | | | |
| | ____________ | | | |
| | ____________ | | | |
| | ____________ | | | |
| Credits: | Voucher Payable | | | |
| | Discounts Earned | | | |

Cheque Number

____________________

Cheque Date

____________________

 Name________________ Date________

## ANSWERS TO SECTION 13.6 EXERCISES (cont.)

**Exercise 4, p. 517**

1. ____________________

2. ____________________

3. ____________________

## ANSWERS TO SECTION 13.7 COMPUTER REVIEW QUESTIONS (text, p. 520)

1. ____________________

2. ____________________

3. ____________________

## COMMUNICATE IT (text, p. 521)

____________________

 Name____________________ Date________________

## ANSWERS TO CHAPTER 13 EXERCISES (text, p. 522)

### USING YOUR KNOWLEDGE

**Exercise 1, p. 522**

## ANSWERS TO CHAPTER 13 EXERCISES (cont.)

**Exercise 2, p. 523**

1. From the audit strip given on p. 523
   1. compute the summary totals that would be produced by the machine;
   2. work out the accounting entry for these totals if the Paid Out is for supplies.

| | | | |
|---|---|---|---|
| | | 137.00 | MDS |
| | | 9.59 | TAX |
| | | 146.59 | TOTL |
| | | 150.00 | CASH |
| CASL | 166 | 3.41 | CHNG |
| | | | |
| | | 175.00 | MDS |
| | | 12.25 | TAX |
| VISA | 167 | 187.25 | TOTL |
| | | | |
| | | 100.00 | RECD |
| RECD | 168 | 100.00 | TOTL |
| | | | |
| | | 356.25 | MDS |
| | | 24.94 | TAX |
| VISA | 169 | 381.19 | TOTL |
| | | | |
| | | REFUND | |
| | | 128.00– | MDS |
| | | 8.96– | TAX |
| | | 136.96– | TOTL |
| CASL | 170 | 136.96– | CASH |
| | | | |
| | | 50.00 | P.O. |
| P.O. | 171 | 50.00 | TOTL |
| | | | |
| | | 150.00 | MDS |
| | | 10.50 | TAX |
| | | 160.50 | TOTL |
| | | 170.00 | CASH |
| CASL | 172 | 9.50 | CHNG |
| | | | |
| | | 70.00 | MDS |
| | | 4.90 | TAX |
| CHRG | 173 | 74.90 | TOTL |

## ANSWERS TO CHAPTER 13 EXERCISES (cont.)

**Ex. 2 (cont.)**

SUMMARY

| | | | |
|---|---|---|---|
| CASL | 174 | ______ | (CASH SALES INCL. TAX) |
| VISA | 175 | ______ | (VISA SALES INCL. TAX) |
| P.O. | 176 | ______ | (PAID OUTS) |
| CHRG | 177 | ______ | (CHRG SALES INCL. TAX) |
| RECD | 178 | ______ | (RECEIVED ON ACCOUNT) |
| CRDT | 179 | ______ | (RETURN FOR CREDIT) |
| TAX | 180 | ______ | (NET SALES TAX) |
| MDS | 181 | ______ | (SALES LESS RETURNS) |
| CASH | 182 | ______ | (NET CASH RECEIVED) |

**2.**

| ACCOUNTS | DR | CR |
|---|---|---|
| | | |
| | | |
| | | |
| | | |
| | | |
| | | |
| | | |

## ANSWERS TO CHAPTER 13 EXERCISES (cont.)

### Exercise 3, p. 523 (Workbook Exercise)

1. Show how each of the items listed to the left below will be dealt with on a bank reconciliation by entering the appropriate letter or symbol in the spaces provided.

| Items | Will be recorded on the reconciliation Y or N | Will be entered on the Bank side (B) or Company Side (C) | Will be recorded as an increase (+) or decrease (–) |
|---|---|---|---|
| a. An NSF cheque appearing in the bank statement and vouchers. Previously not known of by the business. | | | |
| b. A late deposit. | | | |
| c. An outstanding cheque. | | | |
| d. An outstanding cheque from previous reconciliation, cashed in current month. | | | |
| e. An outstanding cheque from previous reconciliation, not cashed in current month. | | | |
| f. A cheque entered incorrectly by business as $95.30; recorded correctly by bank as $93.50. | | | |
| g. Bank service charge not recorded by company. | | | |
| h. An interest charge by the bank in error. | | | |
| i. A certified cheque issued by business but not yet presented by the payee. | | | |
| j. A calculation error by the bank. Balance shown is too large. | | | |

2. How much will the entry be for item "f"?

## ANSWERS TO CHAPTER 13 EXERCISES (cont.)

**Exercise 4, p. 524**

______________________________________________

______________________________________________

______________________________________________

| *Company's Record* | | | *Bank's Record* | | |
|---|---|---|---|---|---|
| | | | | | |
| | | | | | |
| | | | | | |
| | | | | | |
| | | | | | |
| | | | | | |
| | | | | | |
| | | | | | |
| | | | | | |
| | | | | | |
| | | | | | |
| | | | | | |
| | | | | | |
| | | | | | |
| | | | | | |
| | | | | | |
| | | | | | |
| | | | | | |
| | | | | | |
| | | | | | |
| | | | | | |
| | | | | | |
| | | | | | |

 Name________________ Date__________

## ANSWERS TO CHAPTER 13 EXERCISES (cont.)

**Ex. 4 (cont.)**

### GENERAL JOURNAL

PAGE ______

| DATE 19 — | PARTICULARS | P.R. | DEBIT | CREDIT |
|---|---|---|---|---|
| | | | | |

## ANSWERS TO CHAPTER 13 EXERCISES (cont.)

### Exercise 5, p. 527 (Workbook Exercise)

1. From the following records, reconcile the bank account of Baker and Baker as of April 30, 19 —. Record the necessary accounting entries in the books of the business.

   a. Previous bank reconciliation statement.

Baker and Baker
Bank Reconciliation Statement
March 31, 19 —

| | | | | |
|---|---|---|---|---|
| Balance per Bank | | 943.80 | Balance per General Ledger | 305.08 |
| Add Late Deposit | | 216.50 | | |
| | | 1 160.30 | | |
| | | | | |
| Deduct: Outstanding Cheques | | | | |
| # 1207 | $23.01 | | | |
| # 1361 | 14.16 | | | |
| # 1390 | 17.50 | | | |
| # 1406 | 36.71 | | | |
| # 1409 | 19.40 | | | |
| # 1415 | 141.72 | | | |
| # 1420 | 13.16 | | | |
| # 1425 | 51.61 | | | |
| # 1426 | 36.44 | | | |
| # 1428 | 18.19 | | | |
| # 1431 | 76.42 | | | |
| # 1432 | 19.36 | | | |
| # 1433 | 14.40 | | | |
| # 1434 | 85.19 | | | |
| # 1435 | 19.65 | | | |
| # 1436 | 116.40 | | | |
| # 1438 | 78.90 | | | |
| # 1439 | 25.00 | | | |
| # 1440 | 50.00 | 857.22 | | |
| | | 303.08 | | |
| Add: Correction of bank error. Cheque # 1416 for $110.00 was cashed for $112.00 and charged to account for $112.00 | | 2.00 | | |
| True Balance | | 305.08 | True Balance | 305.08 |

## ANSWERS TO CHAPTER 13 EXERCISES (cont.)

**Ex. 5 (cont.)**

**b.** Partial cash payments journal for April, page 17.

| Date | | Chq. No. | Bank CR |
|---|---|---|---|
| 19 — April | 1 | 1441 | 75.92 |
| | 2 | 1442 | 80.00 |
| | 2 | 1443 | 120.00 |
| | 4 | 1444 | 33.71 |
| | 5 | 1445 | 10.00 |
| | 8 | 1446 | 17.50 |
| | 9 | 1447 | 20.10 |
| | 9 | 1448 | 10.00 |
| | 9 | 1449 | 125.00 |
| | 10 | 1450 | 300.00 |
| | 11 | 1451 | 14.77 |
| | 12 | 1452 | 84.33 |
| | 15 | 1453 | 19.06 |
| | 15 | 1454 | 69.50 |
| | 15 | 1455 | 20.00 |
| | 16 | 1456 | 5.61 |
| | 18 | 1457 | 3.20 |
| | 19 | 1458 | 42.75 |
| | 20 | 1459 | 41.00 |
| | 20 | 1460 | 18.30 |
| | 23 | 1461 | 19.00 |
| | 23 | 1462 | 80.00 |
| | 24 | 1463 | 100.00 |
| | 24 | 1464 | 64.70 |
| | 25 | 1465 | 30.00 |
| | 26 | 1466 | 10.00 |
| | 27 | 1467 | 4.50 |
| | 27 | 1468 | 3.50 |
| | 27 | 1469 | 12.00 |
| | 30 | 1470 | 19.00 |
| | 30 | 1471 | 36.00 |
| | 30 | 1472 | 7.85 |
| | | | 1 497.30 |

## ANSWERS TO CHAPTER 13 EXERCISES (cont.)

**Ex. 5 (cont.)**

**c.** "Amount of Deposit" column of cash receipts journal for April, page 8.

| | | |
|---|---|---|
| April | 4 | 216.50 |
| | 10 | 171.41 |
| | 15 | 94.80 |
| | 20 | 156.80 |
| | 24 | 363.85 |
| | 27 | 410.00 |
| | 30 | 94.00 |
| | | 1 507.36 |

**d.** April general journal entry affecting Bank, page 9.

| | Debit | Credit |
|---|---|---|
| Bank | 42.75 | |
| Accounts Payable — C. Brown | | 42.75 |
| To cancel cheque No. 1458 which was issued in error. | | |

**e.** Partial general ledger Bank account.

BANK No. 1

| Date | | Particulars | P.R. | Debit | Credit | Balance | DR CR |
|---|---|---|---|---|---|---|---|
| March | 31 | | | | | 305 08 | DR |
| April | 30 | | CR8 | 1 507 36 | | | |
| | 30 | | CP17 | | 1 497 30 | | |
| | 30 | | J9 | 42 75 | | 357 89 | DR |

## ANSWERS TO CHAPTER 13 EXERCISES (cont.)

**Ex. 5 (cont.)**

**f.** April bank statement.

| Cheques | | | | | Deposits | Date | | Balance |
|---|---|---|---|---|---|---|---|---|
| Balance forwarded | | | | | | Mar | 31 | 943.80 |
| | | | | | 216.50 | Apr | 1 | 1 160.30 |
| 116.40 | (# 1436) | 13.16 | (# 1420) | | | | 2 | 1 030.74 |
| 75.92 | (# 1441) | 17.50 | (# 1390) | | 216.50 | | 4 | |
| 76.42 | (# 1431) | | | | | | 4 | 1 077.40 |
| 19.40 | (# 1409) | 85.19 | (# 1434) | | | | 5 | |
| 10.00 | (# 1445) | | | | | | 5 | 962.81 |
| 18.19 | (# 1428) | | | | | | 8 | 944.62 |
| 36.71 | (# 1406) | 50.00 | (# 1440) | | 171.41 | | 10 | |
| 25.00 | (# 1439) | 120.00 | (# 1443) | | | | 10 | |
| 300.00 | (# 1450) | | | | | | 10 | 584.32 |
| 14.40 | (# 1433) | | | | | | 11 | 569.92 |
| 78.90 | (# 1438) | 80.00 | (# 1442) | | | | 15 | |
| 20.00 | (# 1455) | 20.10 | (# 1447) | | | | 15 | 370.92 |
| 141.72 | (# 1415) | | | | 94.80 | | 16 | 324.00 |
| 51.61 | (# 1425) | 125.00 | (# 1449) | | | | 18 | 147.39 |
| | | | (Correct March Error) | | 2.00 | | 19 | 149.39 |
| | | | | | 156.80 | | 20 | 306.19 |
| 36.44 | (# 1426) | 84.33 | (# 1452) | | | | 23 | |
| 18.30 | (# 1460) | | | | | | 23 | 167.12 |
| 100.00 | (# 1463) | | | | 363.85 | | 24 | 430.97 |
| 19.65 | (# 1435) | 16.09 | (# 1453) | | | | 25 | 395.23 |
| | | | | | 410.00 | | 27 | 805.23 |
| DM 5.60 | (Service Charge) | | | | | | 27 | 799.63 |
| INT 36.00 | (Interest on Loan) | | | | | | 30 | 763.63 |
| DM 250.00 | (Loan Reduction) | | | | | | 30 | 513.63 |
| | | | | | 100.00 | | 30 | 613.63 |
| 3.20 | (# 1457) | 4.50 | (# 1467) | | | | 30 | 605.93 |

## ANSWERS TO CHAPTER 13 EXERCISES (cont.)

**Ex. 5 (cont.)**

| Company's Record | | | | | | Bank's Record | | | | | |
|---|---|---|---|---|---|---|---|---|---|---|---|

## ANSWERS TO CHAPTER 13 EXERCISES (cont.)

**Ex. 5 (cont.)**

### GENERAL JOURNAL PAGE

| DATE 19 — | | PARTICULARS | P.R. | DEBIT | CREDIT |
|---|---|---|---|---|---|
| | | | | | |
| | | | | | |
| | | | | | |
| | | | | | |
| | | | | | |
| | | | | | |
| | | | | | |
| | | | | | |
| | | | | | |
| | | | | | |

**Exercise 6, p. 527 (Workbook Exercise)**

From the following records, prepare the bank reconciliation statement for Madison Company as of October 31, 19 —. Record the necessary accounting entries in the books of the business.

**a.** Previous bank reconciliation statement

*Madison Company*
*Bank Reconciliation Statement*
*September 30, 19 —*

| | | | | | |
|---|---|---|---|---|---|
| *Bal. per Bk. Statement* | | 2 102 69 | *Bal. per General Ledger* | | 1 652 95 |
| *Deduct: Outstanding Cheques* | | | *Deduct: Service Charge* | $12.50 | |
| # 519 | $ 20.00 | | *Loan Interest* | 36.25 | 48 75 |
| # 526 | 37.50 | | | | |
| # 528 | 105.00 | | | | |
| # 529 | 2.70 | | | | |
| # 531 | 5.19 | | | | |
| # 532 | 74.10 | | | | |
| # 533 | 112.02 | | | | |
| # 534 | 56.94 | | | | |
| # 535 | 85.04 | 498 49 | | | |
| *True Balance* | | 1 604 20 | *True Balance* | | 1 604 20 |

 Name________________ Date________

## ANSWERS TO CHAPTER 13 EXERCISES (cont.)

**Ex. 6 (cont.)**

**b.** Partial cash payments journal.

Page 174

| Date | | Ch. No. | Bank Cr | |
|---|---|---|---|---|
| 19— Oct | 1 | 536 | 19 | 05 |
| | 1 | 537 | 164 | 02 |
| | 2 | 538 | 73 | 74 |
| | 3 | 539 | 27 | 60 |
| | 3 | 540 | 1 | 95 |
| | 4 | 541 | 365 | 12 |
| | 5 | 542 | 92 | 06 |
| | 8 | 543 | 74 | 09 |
| | 8 | 544 | 19 | 65 |
| | 10 | 545 | 74 | 02 |
| | 11 | 546 | 76 | 75 |
| | 12 | 547 | 56 | 21 |
| | 12 | 548 | 42 | 96 |
| | 15 | 549 | 33 | 21 |
| | 17 | 550 | 24 | 02 |
| | 19 | 551 | 88 | 61 |
| | 22 | 552 | 58 | 36 |
| | 22 | 553 | 19 | 05 |
| | 23 | 554 | 91 | 50 |
| | 24 | 555 | 13 | 30 |
| | 24 | 556 | 17 | 50 |
| | 26 | 557 | 8 | 61 |
| | 29 | 558 | 1 047 | 65 |
| | 29 | 559 | 319 | 02 |
| | 30 | 560 | 1 | 75 |
| | 31 | 561 | 2 | 50 |
| | 31 | 562 | 19 | 41 |
| | | | 2 831 | 71 |

**c.** Partial cash receipts journal.

Page 147

| Date | | Bank Dr | | Amount of Deposit | |
|---|---|---|---|---|---|
| 19— Oct | 3 | 16 | 50 | | |
| | 3 | 25 | 02 | | |
| | 3 | 516 | 95 | 558 | 47 |
| | 8 | 104 | 20 | | |
| | 8 | 756 | 12 | | |
| | 8 | 56 | 12 | | |
| | 8 | 96 | 02 | 1 012 | 46 |
| | 11 | 33 | 40 | 33 | 40 |
| | 15 | 17 | 50 | | |
| | 15 | 12 | 09 | 29 | 59 |
| | 22 | 19 | 06 | | |
| | 22 | 502 | 00 | 521 | 06 |
| | 24 | 12 | 06 | | |
| | 24 | 13 | 50 | | |
| | 24 | 91 | 02 | | |
| | 24 | 16 | 51 | 133 | 09 |
| | 29 | 56 | 93 | | |
| | 29 | 83 | 16 | | |
| | 29 | 102 | 52 | | |
| | 29 | 127 | 06 | | |
| | 29 | 31 | 50 | 401 | 17 |
| | 31 | 167 | 75 | | |
| | 31 | 138 | 44 | 306 | 19 |
| | | 2 995 | 43 | 2 995 | 43 |

## ANSWERS TO CHAPTER 13 EXERCISES (cont.)

**Ex. 6 (cont.)**

**d.** October general journal entry affecting Bank.

GENERAL JOURNAL PAGE 64

| DATE 19— | | PARTICULARS | P.R. | DEBIT | CREDIT |
|---|---|---|---|---|---|
| Oct. | 4 | Bank Charges | 54 | 12 50 | |
| | | Bank Interest | 56 | 36 25 | |
| | | Bank | | | 48 75 |
| | | To record charges picked up from September | | | |
| | | bank statement | | | |

**e.** Bank statement for October.

| Cheques | | | | Deposits | Date | | Balance |
|---|---|---|---|---|---|---|---|
| | | | | | Sept | 30 | 2 102.69 |
| 37.50 | (526) | | | | Oct | 2 | 2 065.19 |
| | | | | 558.47 | | 3 | 2 623.66 |
| 2.70 | (529) | 85.04 | (535) | | | 4 | 2 535.92 |
| 19.05 | (536) | | | | | 5 | 2 516.87 |
| 74.10 | (532) | 105.00 | (528) | | | 8 | 2 337.77 |
| 73.74 | (538) | | | 1 012.46 | | 9 | 3 276.49 |
| 5.19 | (531) | 27.60 | (539) | | | 10 | 3 243.70 |
| 56.94 | (534) | | | | | 11 | 3 186.76 |
| 74.09 | (543) | 112.02 | (533) | 33.40 | | 15 | 3 034.05 |
| 96.02 | (N.S.F. cheque of J. Marble) | | | | | 15 | 2 938.03 |
| 164.02 | (537) | | | | | 16 | 2 774.01 |
| 33.21 | (549) | 19.65 | (544) | 29.59 | | 17 | 2 750.74 |
| 365.12 | (541) | | | | | 18 | 2 385.62 |
| 76.75 | (546) | | | 521.06 | | 22 | 2 829.93 |
| 1.95 | (540) | 58.36 | (552) | | | 23 | 2 769.62 |
| 42.96 | (548) | | | | | 24 | 2 726.66 |
| | | | | 133.09 | | 25 | 2 859.75 |
| 88.61 | (551) | | | | | 26 | 2 771.14 |
| 91.50 | (554) | | | | | 29 | 2 679.64 |
| 13.30 | (555) | | | 401.17 | | 30 | 3 067.51 |
| 8.61 | (557) | 1 047.65 | (558) | | | 31 | 2 011.25 |
| 15.20 | (Int) | 30.20 | (Service Charges) | | | 31 | 1 965.85 |
| 43.50 | (Discount Fee) | | | | | 31 | 1922.35 |

## ANSWERS TO CHAPTER 13 EXERCISES (cont.)

**Ex. 6 (cont.)**

**f.** General ledger account showing October figures.

ACCOUNT *Bank* No. *1*

| DATE 19— | | PARTICULARS | P.R. | DEBIT | CREDIT | Dr Cr | BALANCE |
|---|---|---|---|---|---|---|---|
| Sept | 30 | | — | | | DR | 1 6 5 2 95 |
| Oct | 4 | | J64 | | 4 8 75 | | |
| | 31 | | CP174 | | 2 8 3 1 71 | | |
| | 31 | | CR147 | 2 9 9 5 43 | | DR | 1 7 6 7 92 |

| Company's Record | | Bank's Record | |
|---|---|---|---|
| | | | |

## ANSWERS TO CHAPTER 13 EXERCISES (cont.)

**Ex. 6 (cont.)**

### GENERAL JOURNAL

PAGE ________

| DATE 19 — | | PARTICULARS | P.R. | DEBIT | CREDIT |
|---|---|---|---|---|---|
| | | | | | |
| | | | | | |
| | | | | | |
| | | | | | |
| | | | | | |
| | | | | | |
| | | | | | |
| | | | | | |
| | | | | | |

**Exercise 7, p. 527**

1. a. Cash means dollar bills and coins only.
   b. The principal objective of a business is to earn a profit.
   c. The usual method of establishing a petty cash fund is to issue a cheque made out to Petty Cash.
   d. The imprest system of petty cash involves entrusting the cash to an individual.
   e. The vouchers and the cash in the petty cash box should add up to the balance of the Petty Cash account.

   ☐

2. a. The cheque made out to Petty Cash is usually handed over to the person responsible for the petty cash fund.
   b. Outside of office hours the petty cash box is usually kept in the company safe.
   c. For every expenditure out of the petty cash fund there must be a bill or sales slip from a store.
   d. When a payment is being made out of the petty cash fund, no accounting entries are made immediately.
   e. The petty cash fund must be replenished when the amount of cash in the box gets low.

   ☐

## ANSWERS TO CHAPTER 13 EXERCISES (cont.)

**Ex. 7 (cont.)**

**3.** a. The first step to replenishing the petty cash fund is to prepare a summary of the vouchers in the petty cash box. ☐
b. The petty cashier submits the summary of charges, together with the bills and vouchers in order to obtain a cheque.
c. The summary and the vouchers together are accepted as the source document for the replenishing cheque.
d. The accounting entry to record the replenishing cheque is: debit Petty Cash; credit Bank.
e. The accounting entry to replenish the petty cash fund is one of the two accounting entries that affect petty cash.

**4.** a. Banks provide essential services for both businesses and individuals. ☐
b. The processing of cheques and bank credit card vouchers is known as the electronic transfer of funds.
c. Banks are able to meet the needs of most customers by having a variety of accounts and services.
d. The interest rate for a daily interest savings account is higher than it is for a pure savings account.
e. You must put some money in a bank account to "open" it.

**5.** a. The bank statement given to the customer once a month is identical to the bank's own record. ☐
b. Except for breakdowns, electronic tellers may be used at any time.
c. It is difficult to borrow money if your credit rating is poor.
d. Writing cheques that bounce can be damaging to your credit rating.
e. The true bank balance is the one shown by the bank's record.

**6.** a. Placing only your signature on the back of a cheque made out to you is an "open" endorsement. ☐
b. Banks require the payee (the person to whom the cheque is issued) to guarantee the cheque by signing it on the back.
c. If the balance in the issuer's account is not large enough to cover the amount of a cheque, the bank will dishonour it.
d. A cheque that has not bounced is a dishonoured cheque.
e. The bank has the right to take the amount of a dishonoured cheque out of your account without contacting you.

**7.** a. The accounting entry to record a dishonoured cheque is the exact opposite of the accounting entry that was made when the cheque was deposited. ☐
b. You must phone the bank to find out if a cheque that you received is certified.
c. You can be sure of a cheque not bouncing if it is certified.
d. The funds to pay a certified cheque are taken out of the bank account at the time the cheque is certified.
e. A post-dated cheque is one that is dated for some time in the future.

## ANSWERS TO CHAPTER 13 EXERCISES (cont.)

**Ex. 7 (cont.)**

**8.** a. The usual reason for issuing a post-dated cheque is to meet a series of payments such as for a mortgage. ☐
b. A certified cheque is marked GUARANTEED by the bank.
c. A cheque written on January 15 but dated for March 1 is a post-dated cheque.
d. You should ask for a certified cheque when you are dealing with a stranger and when the amount of money is large.
e. The bank does not cash cheques bearing a future date.

**9.** a. Bank credit cards can be obtained from large department stores and similar chains. ☐
b. Most smaller retail outlets do not offer their own individualized credit cards.
c. Visa and Mastercard are bank credit cards sponsored by major banks.
d. The consumer is usually given twenty-one days from the statement to make payment.
e. Bank credit cards may be used to obtain a cash advance.

**10.** a. The bank credit card system depends on computerized equipment to make it work. ☐
b. The consumer's credit rating is established with a merchant when the credit card is presented.
c. For some purchases it is better to take an ordinary bank loan than to use the bank credit card.
d. Credit card slips are deposited in the bank just as if they were cheques from customers.
e. The consumer pays all of the charges made by the banks for the bank credit card system.

**11.** a. A listing of cheques received in the mail is prepared because the cheques have to be deposited in the bank. ☐
b. The listing of the cheques in part **a** is prepared by a member of the accounting department who knows the system.
c. Sales slips are pre-numbered so that all slips can be accounted for.
d. In a business where there are "cash" receipts, it is necessary to prove the cash at the end of each day.
e. There is a greater chance for a cash shortage than there is for a cash overage.

**12.** a. A point-of-sale terminal is a stand-alone electronic cash register. ☐
b. A "float" is a small sum of money set aside to be used as a starting fund for the cash register each day.
c. The detailed audit tape is locked inside the cash register.
d. At the end of each day the cash register can be made to produce summary totals for the day.
e. A modern cash register can itself produce most of the figures needed to prove the cash.

## ANSWERS TO CHAPTER 13 EXERCISES (cont.)

**Ex. 7 (cont.)**

**13.** a. At the end of each day the cash, vouchers, and daily balance form are forwarded to the accounting department.
b. A cash shortage is entered as a debit to an expense account.
c. A current bank account is designed specially for the use of businesses.
d. With a current account the paid cheques are returned to the depositor at the end of each month.
e. Cash is said to be proved when there is no shortage or overage.

**14.** a. Businesses endorse all cheques "For Deposit Only."
b. All cheques for deposit must be endorsed.
c. For businesses, deposit slips are prepared in duplicate.
d. Every business requires internal control to ensure accuracy and honesty.
e. The person who records transactions or prepares accounting records should not also be the one to control or handle the assets physically.

**15.** a. Cash is the single item most likely to be stolen.
b. The total cash receipts for the day should be deposited on that day and intact.
c. Since both the bank and the business keep a record of the same funds, the two balances should always agree unless an error has been made.
d. Every bank account should be reconciled once a month.
e. An outstanding cheque is a cheque that is issued and recorded by the company but not cashed by the bank.

**FOR FURTHER THOUGHT**

**Exercise 8, p. 529**

1. ____________________

2. ____________________

3. ____________________

4. ____________________

5. ____________________

6. ____________________

## ANSWERS TO CHAPTER 13 EXERCISES (cont.)

**Ex. 8 (cont.)**

**7.** ______________________________

**8.** ______________________________

**9.** ______________________________

## CASE STUDIES (text, p. 530)

**Case 1** *Service Charges: Are They Always Fair?*, p. 530

**1.** ______________________________

**2.** ______________________________

**3.** ______________________________

**4.** ______________________________

**Case 2** *Trials of a Young Entrepreneur*, p. 531

**1.** ______________________________

**2.** ______________________________

**3.** ______________________________

**4.** ______________________________

**5.** ______________________________

**6.** ______________________________

**7.** ______________________________

## CASE STUDIES (cont.)

### Case 2 (cont.)

8. ______________________

### Case 3 *The Good Life on Plastic Money*, p. 532

1. ______________________
2. ______________________
3. ______________________
4. ______________________
5. ______________________

### Case 4 *Is Opportunity Knocking?*, p. 533

______________________

 Name________________ Date________________

## CASE STUDIES (cont.)

**Case 4 (cont.)**

## CAREER David Nagashima/Regional Bank Manager

### ANSWERS TO DISCUSSION QUESTIONS (text, p. 536)

1.

| Positions | Accounting Knowledge Required | Education Programs Completed |
|---|---|---|
| Management Trainee | | Bachelor of Commerce |
| Account Executive | | |
| Project Manager | | |
| Bank Manager | | |
| Regional Manager | | |
| Vice-president | | |

2. ________________

3. ________________

## ANSWERS TO DISCUSSION QUESTIONS (cont.)

4. ______________________________

5. ______________________________

6. ______________________________

7. ______________________________

## SUPPLEMENTARY EXERCISE (text, p. 537)

### Green Thumb Garden Centre

PURCHASES JOURNAL

Page 77

| DATE 19— | NAME | OTHER ACCOUNTS DR. | | | | | Trucks Expense DR | Soil Prep + Mtce. DR | Equipment Expense DR | Purchases DR | Accounts Payable CR |
|---|---|---|---|---|---|---|---|---|---|---|---|
| | | ACCOUNT | P.R. | AMOUNT | | | | | | | |
| | | | | | | | | | | | |

 Name________________ Date________________

**Supplementary Exercise (cont.)**

CASH PAYMENTS JOURNAL

Page 47

| DATE 19— | NAME | OTHER ACCOUNTS DR. | | | Wages DR | G.O.E. Drawings DR | Soil Prep + Mtce. DR | Discounts Earned CR | Accounts Payable DR | Bank CR | Cheque No. |
|---|---|---|---|---|---|---|---|---|---|---|---|
| | | ACCOUNT | P.R. | AMOUNT | | | | | | | |

# Green Thumb

Name________________________ Date________________

**Supplementary Exercise (cont.)**

CASH PAYMENTS JOURNAL

Page 47

| DATE 19— | NAME | OTHER ACCOUNTS DR. | | | Wages DR | G.O.E. Drawings DR | Soil Prep + Mtce. DR | Discounts Earned CR | Accounts Payable DR | Bank CR | Cheque No. |
|---|---|---|---|---|---|---|---|---|---|---|---|
| | | ACCOUNT | P.R. | AMOUNT | | | | | | | |
| | | | | | | | | | | | |

 Name________________________ Date__________

Supplementary Exercise (cont.)

CASH RECEIPTS JOURNAL

Page 65

| DATE 19— | | NAME | OTHER ACCOUNTS CR. | | | Cash Short and Over DR | Discounts Allowed DR | Sales Tax Payable CR | Sales CR | Accounts Receivable DR | Accounts Receivable CR | Bank DR |
|---|---|---|---|---|---|---|---|---|---|---|---|---|
| | | | ACCOUNT | P.R. | AMOUNT | | | | | | | |

# Green Thumb

Name________________________ Date________________

**Supplementary Exercise (cont.)**

CASH RECEIPTS JOURNAL

Page 65

| DATE 19 — | NAME | OTHER ACCOUNTS CR. | | | Cash Short and Over DR | Discounts Allowed DR | Sales Tax Payable CR | Sales CR | Accounts Receivable DR | Accounts Receivable CR | Bank DR |
|---|---|---|---|---|---|---|---|---|---|---|---|
| | | ACCOUNT | P.R. | AMOUNT | | | | | | | |

**Supplementary Exercise (cont.)**

## GENERAL LEDGER ACCOUNTS

**ACCOUNT** Petty Cash **NO.** 105

| DATE 19— | | PARTICULARS | P.R. | DEBIT | CREDIT | D/C | BALANCE |
|---|---|---|---|---|---|---|---|
| May | 31 | Balance Forwarded | – | | | DR | 100 – |
| | | | | | | | |
| | | | | | | | |
| | | | | | | | |

**ACCOUNT** Bank **NO.** 110

| DATE 19— | | PARTICULARS | P.R. | DEBIT | CREDIT | D/C | BALANCE |
|---|---|---|---|---|---|---|---|
| May | 31 | Balance Forwarded | — | | | DR | 3527 24 |
| | | | | | | | |
| | | | | | | | |
| | | | | | | | |

**ACCOUNT** Accounts Receivable **NO.** 115

| DATE 19— | | PARTICULARS | P.R. | DEBIT | CREDIT | D/C | BALANCE |
|---|---|---|---|---|---|---|---|
| May | 31 | Balance Forwarded | — | | | DR | 1925 18 |
| | | | | | | | |
| | | | | | | | |
| | | | | | | | |

## Green Thumb

Name ____________________ Date ____________

**Supplementary Exercise (cont.)**

**ACCOUNT** Merchandise Inventory **NO.** 120

| DATE 19— | | PARTICULARS | P.R. | DEBIT | CREDIT | D/C | BALANCE |
|---|---|---|---|---|---|---|---|
| May | 31 | Balance Forwarded | — | | | DR | 75 746 53 |
| | | | | | | | |
| | | | | | | | |
| | | | | | | | |

**ACCOUNT** Supplies **NO.** 125

| DATE 19— | | PARTICULARS | P.R. | DEBIT | CREDIT | D/C | BALANCE |
|---|---|---|---|---|---|---|---|
| May | 31 | Balance Forwarded | — | | | DR | 595 – |
| | | | | | | | |
| | | | | | | | |
| | | | | | | | |

**ACCOUNT** Land **NO.** 130

| DATE 19— | | PARTICULARS | P.R. | DEBIT | CREDIT | D/C | BALANCE |
|---|---|---|---|---|---|---|---|
| May | 31 | Balance Forwarded | — | | | DR | 48 000 – |
| | | | | | | | |
| | | | | | | | |
| | | | | | | | |

**ACCOUNT** Buildings **NO.** 135

| DATE 19— | | PARTICULARS | P.R. | DEBIT | CREDIT | D/C | BALANCE |
|---|---|---|---|---|---|---|---|
| May | 31 | Balance Forwarded | — | | | DR | 65 500 – |
| | | | | | | | |

## Green Thumb

Name ________________ Date ________________

**Supplementary Exercise (cont.)**

**ACCOUNT** Trucks and Tractors **NO.** 145

| DATE 19— | | PARTICULARS | P.R. | DEBIT | CREDIT | D/C | BALANCE |
|---|---|---|---|---|---|---|---|
| May | 31 | Balance Forwarded | — | | | DR | 40 500 — |
| | | | | | | | |

**ACCOUNT** Bank Loan **NO.** 205

| DATE 19— | | PARTICULARS | P.R. | DEBIT | CREDIT | D/C | BALANCE |
|---|---|---|---|---|---|---|---|
| May | 31 | Balance Forwarded | — | | | CR | 20 000 — |
| | | | | | | | |
| | | | | | | | |
| | | | | | | | |

**ACCOUNT** Accounts Payable **NO.** 210

| DATE 19— | | PARTICULARS | P.R. | DEBIT | CREDIT | D/C | BALANCE |
|---|---|---|---|---|---|---|---|
| May | 31 | Balance Forwarded | — | | | CR | 7 861 87 |
| | | | | | | | |
| | | | | | | | |
| | | | | | | | |

**ACCOUNT** Sales Tax Payable **NO.** 215

| DATE 19— | | PARTICULARS | P.R. | DEBIT | CREDIT | D/C | BALANCE |
|---|---|---|---|---|---|---|---|
| May | 31 | Balance Forwarded | — | | | CR | 2 195 45 |
| | | | | | | | |
| | | | | | | | |
| | | | | | | | |

**Supplementary Exercise (cont.)**

**ACCOUNT** Mortgage Payable **NO.** 220

| DATE 19— | | PARTICULARS | P.R. | DEBIT | CREDIT | D/C | BALANCE |
|---|---|---|---|---|---|---|---|
| May | 31 | Balance Forwarded | — | | | CR | 45 500 – |
| | | | | | | | |
| | | | | | | | |
| | | | | | | | |

**ACCOUNT** G.O. Emms, Capital **NO.** 305

| DATE 19— | | PARTICULARS | P.R. | DEBIT | CREDIT | D/C | BALANCE |
|---|---|---|---|---|---|---|---|
| May | 31 | Balance Forwarded | — | | | CR | 176 415 91 |
| | | | | | | | |
| | | | | | | | |
| | | | | | | | |

**ACCOUNT** G.O. Emms, Drawings **NO.** 310

| DATE 19— | | PARTICULARS | P.R. | DEBIT | CREDIT | D/C | BALANCE |
|---|---|---|---|---|---|---|---|
| May | 31 | Balance Forwarded | – | | | DR | 15 654 60 |
| | | | | | | | |
| | | | | | | | |
| | | | | | | | |

**ACCOUNT** Sales **NO.** 405

| DATE 19— | | PARTICULARS | P.R. | DEBIT | CREDIT | D/C | BALANCE |
|---|---|---|---|---|---|---|---|
| May | 31 | Balance Forwarded | — | | | CR | 45 042 19 |
| | | | | | | | |
| | | | | | | | |
| | | | | | | | |

# Green Thumb

Name ______________________ Date ______________

**Supplementary Exercise (cont.)**

**ACCOUNT** Bank Charges **NO.** 505

| DATE 19— | | PARTICULARS | P.R. | DEBIT | CREDIT | D/C | BALANCE |
|---|---|---|---|---|---|---|---|
| May | 31 | Balance Forwarded | — | | | DR | 5 4 7 53 |
| | | | | | | | |
| | | | | | | | |
| | | | | | | | |

**ACCOUNT** Building Repairs **NO.** 510

| DATE 19— | | PARTICULARS | P.R. | DEBIT | CREDIT | D/C | BALANCE |
|---|---|---|---|---|---|---|---|
| May | 31 | Balance Forwarded | – | | | DR | 1 4 6 51 |
| | | | | | | | |
| | | | | | | | |
| | | | | | | | |

**ACCOUNT** Cash Short and Over **NO.** 515

| DATE 19— | | PARTICULARS | P.R. | DEBIT | CREDIT | D/C | BALANCE |
|---|---|---|---|---|---|---|---|
| May | 31 | Balance Forwarded | — | | | DR | 1 0 50 |
| | | | | | | | |
| | | | | | | | |
| | | | | | | | |

**ACCOUNT** Discounts Allowed **NO.** 520

| DATE 19— | | PARTICULARS | P.R. | DEBIT | CREDIT | D/C | BALANCE |
|---|---|---|---|---|---|---|---|
| May | 31 | Balance Forwarded | — | | | DR | 9 5 75 |
| | | | | | | | |
| | | | | | | | |
| | | | | | | | |

## Green Thumb

Name ______________________ Date ______________

**Supplementary Exercise (cont.)**

**ACCOUNT** Discounts Earned **NO.** 525

| DATE 19— | | PARTICULARS | P.R. | DEBIT | CREDIT | D/C | BALANCE |
|---|---|---|---|---|---|---|---|
| May | 31 | Balance Forwarded | — | | | CR | 5 4 70 |
| | | | | | | | |
| | | | | | | | |
| | | | | | | | |

**ACCOUNT** Equipment Expense **NO.** 530

| DATE 19— | | PARTICULARS | P.R. | DEBIT | CREDIT | D/C | BALANCE |
|---|---|---|---|---|---|---|---|
| May | 31 | Balance Forwarded | — | | | DR | 5 0 6 86 |
| | | | | | | | |
| | | | | | | | |
| | | | | | | | |

**ACCOUNT** Freight-in **NO.** 535

| DATE 19— | | PARTICULARS | P.R. | DEBIT | CREDIT | D/C | BALANCE |
|---|---|---|---|---|---|---|---|
| May | 31 | Balance Forwarded | — | | | DR | 8 5 6 60 |
| | | | | | | | |
| | | | | | | | |
| | | | | | | | |

**ACCOUNT** Light, Heat, and Power **NO.** 540

| DATE 19— | | PARTICULARS | P.R. | DEBIT | CREDIT | D/C | BALANCE |
|---|---|---|---|---|---|---|---|
| May | 31 | Balance Forwarded | — | | | DR | 1 3 0 6 75 |
| | | | | | | | |
| | | | | | | | |
| | | | | | | | |

## Green Thumb

Name ____________________ Date ____________________

**Supplementary Exercise (cont.)**

**ACCOUNT** Miscellaneous Expense **NO.** 545

| DATE 19— | | PARTICULARS | P.R. | DEBIT | CREDIT | D/C | BALANCE |
|---|---|---|---|---|---|---|---|
| May | 31 | Balance Forwarded | — | | | DR | 1 9 2 45 |
| | | | | | | | |
| | | | | | | | |
| | | | | | | | |
| | | | | | | | |
| | | | | | | | |
| | | | | | | | |
| | | | | | | | |

**ACCOUNT** Purchases **NO.** 550

| DATE 19— | | PARTICULARS | P.R. | DEBIT | CREDIT | D/C | BALANCE |
|---|---|---|---|---|---|---|---|
| May | 31 | Balance Forwarded | — | | | DR | 30 0 0 1 05 |
| | | | | | | | |
| | | | | | | | |
| | | | | | | | |

**ACCOUNT** Soil Preparation and Maintenance **NO.** 555

| DATE 19— | | PARTICULARS | P.R. | DEBIT | CREDIT | D/C | BALANCE |
|---|---|---|---|---|---|---|---|
| May | 31 | Balance Forwarded | — | | | DR | 4 8 5 8 25 |
| | | | | | | | |
| | | | | | | | |
| | | | | | | | |

**Supplementary Exercise (cont.)**

**ACCOUNT** Telephone **NO.** 560

| DATE 19— | | PARTICULARS | P.R. | DEBIT | CREDIT | D/C | BALANCE |
|---|---|---|---|---|---|---|---|
| May | 31 | Balance Forwarded | – | | | DR | 519 42 |
| | | | | | | | |
| | | | | | | | |
| | | | | | | | |

**ACCOUNT** Truck Expense **NO.** 565

| DATE 19— | | PARTICULARS | P.R. | DEBIT | CREDIT | D/C | BALANCE |
|---|---|---|---|---|---|---|---|
| May | 31 | Balance Forwarded | — | | | DR | 2 104 40 |
| | | | | | | | |
| | | | | | | | |
| | | | | | | | |

**ACCOUNT** Wages **NO.** 570

| DATE 19— | | PARTICULARS | P.R. | DEBIT | CREDIT | D/C | BALANCE |
|---|---|---|---|---|---|---|---|
| May | 31 | Balance Forwarded | – | | | DR | 4 375 50 |
| | | | | | | | |
| | | | | | | | |
| | | | | | | | |

## ACCOUNTS RECEIVABLE LEDGER

**ACCOUNT** F. Carson & Sons 2% 10 : n30 **NO.**

| DATE 19— | | PARTICULARS | P.R. | DEBIT | CREDIT | D/C | BALANCE |
|---|---|---|---|---|---|---|---|
| May | 31 | Forwarded # 408 of May 30 | — | | | DR | 541 80 |
| | | | | | | | |
| | | | | | | | |
| | | | | | | | |

 Name_______________ Date__________

**Supplementary Exercise (cont.)**

ACCOUNT C. Swinton 2%10 : n 30 NO.

| DATE 19— | | PARTICULARS | P.R. | DEBIT | CREDIT | D/C | BALANCE |
|---|---|---|---|---|---|---|---|
| May | 31 | Forwarded # 407 of May 26 | — | | | DR | 1 0 9 4 63 |
| | | | | | | | |
| | | | | | | | |
| | | | | | | | |
| | | | | | | | |
| | | | | | | | |
| | | | | | | | |

ACCOUNT Varga Brothers 2% 10 : n 30 NO.

| DATE 19— | | PARTICULARS | P.R. | DEBIT | CREDIT | D/C | BALANCE |
|---|---|---|---|---|---|---|---|
| May | 31 | Forwarded # 402 of May 24 | — | | | DR | 2 8 8 75 |
| | | | | | | | |
| | | | | | | | |
| | | | | | | | |
| | | | | | | | |
| | | | | | | | |
| | | | | | | | |

# Green Thumb

Name______________________ Date______________

**Supplementary Exercise (cont.)**

## ACCOUNTS PAYABLE LEDGER

**ACCOUNT** Acorn Seed Terms 2/15, n/30 **NO.**

| DATE 19— | | PARTICULARS | P.R. | DEBIT | CREDIT | D/C | BALANCE |
|---|---|---|---|---|---|---|---|
| May | 31 | Fwd. # 654, May 18, $147; # 672, May 21, $317.10 | — | | | CR | 464 10 |
| | | | | | | | |
| | | | | | | | |
| | | | | | | | |
| | | | | | | | |
| | | | | | | | |
| | | | | | | | |

**ACCOUNT** City Gas and Oil Terms Net 30 **NO.**

| DATE 19— | | PARTICULARS | P.R. | DEBIT | CREDIT | D/C | BALANCE |
|---|---|---|---|---|---|---|---|
| | | | | | | | |
| | | | | | | | |
| | | | | | | | |
| | | | | | | | |

**Supplementary Exercise (cont.)**

**ACCOUNT** Clay Ceramic Co. Terms Net 45 **NO.**

| DATE 19— | | PARTICULARS | P.R. | DEBIT | CREDIT | D/C | BALANCE |
|---|---|---|---|---|---|---|---|
| May | 31 | Fwd. # 1701, Apr. 24 | — | | | CR | 5 4 0 75 |
| | | | | | | | |
| | | | | | | | |
| | | | | | | | |
| | | | | | | | |
| | | | | | | | |
| | | | | | | | |

**ACCOUNT** Canada Products Terms Net 30 **NO.**

| DATE 19— | | PARTICULARS | P.R. | DEBIT | CREDIT | D/C | BALANCE |
|---|---|---|---|---|---|---|---|
| May | 31 | Fwd. # B160 May 4 $58.80 # B188 May 12 $98.91 # B249 May 30 $35.91 | — | | | CR | 1 9 3 62 |
| | | | | | | | |
| | | | | | | | |
| | | | | | | | |
| | | | | | | | |
| | | | | | | | |
| | | | | | | | |

# Green Thumb

Name____________________ Date____________

**Supplementary Exercise (cont.)**

**ACCOUNT** Equipment Repair and Supply Terms Net 30 **NO.**

| DATE 19— | | PARTICULARS | P.R. | DEBIT | CREDIT | D/C | BALANCE |
|---|---|---|---|---|---|---|---|
| | | | | | | | |
| | | | | | | | |
| | | | | | | | |
| | | | | | | | |

**ACCOUNT** Kemp Haulage Terms 1/10, n/30 **NO.**

| DATE 19— | | PARTICULARS | P.R. | DEBIT | CREDIT | D/C | BALANCE |
|---|---|---|---|---|---|---|---|
| | | Fwd. #747 May 23 $52.50; #754 May 23 $52.50; #760 May 23 $52.50; #772 May 27 $52.50; #795 May 31 $78.75 | — | | | CR | 288.75 |
| | | | | | | | |
| | | | | | | | |
| | | | | | | | |
| | | | | | | | |
| | | | | | | | |
| | | | | | | | |

**ACCOUNT** M. & M. Chemicals Terms Net 60 **NO.**

| DATE 19— | | PARTICULARS | P.R. | DEBIT | CREDIT | D/C | BALANCE |
|---|---|---|---|---|---|---|---|
| May | 31 | Fwd. #104b Apr 9 | — | | | CR | 1932 – |
| | | | | | | | |
| | | | | | | | |
| | | | | | | | |

**Supplementary Exercise (cont.)**

ACCOUNT Poplar Finance NO.

| DATE 19— | | PARTICULARS | P.R. | DEBIT | CREDIT | D/C | BALANCE |
|---|---|---|---|---|---|---|---|
| May | 31 | Forwarded | — | | | CR | 2560 – |
| | | | | | | | |
| | | | | | | | |
| | | | | | | | |

ACCOUNT Sylvester Concrete Terms Net 30 NO.

| DATE 19— | | PARTICULARS | P.R. | DEBIT | CREDIT | D/C | BALANCE |
|---|---|---|---|---|---|---|---|
| May | 31 | Forwarded #446 May 5 | — | | | CR | 783 51 |
| | | | | | | | |
| | | | | | | | |
| | | | | | | | |

ACCOUNT Triangle Sod Terms Net 30 NO.

| DATE 19— | | PARTICULARS | P.R. | DEBIT | CREDIT | D/C | BALANCE |
|---|---|---|---|---|---|---|---|
| May | 31 | Forwarded #374 May 22 | — | | | CR | 1099 14 |
| | | | | | | | |
| | | | | | | | |
| | | | | | | | |
| | | | | | | | |
| | | | | | | | |
| | | | | | | | |

# Green Thumb

Name______________________ Date______________

**Supplementary Exercise (cont.)**

*Green Thumb Garden Centre*

*General Ledger Trial Balance*

*June 30, 19—*

| | | | DR | CR |
|---|---|---|---|---|

**Supplementary Exercise (cont.)**

Green Thumb Garden Centre
Accounts Receivable Schedule
June 30, 19 –

Green Thumb Garden Centre
Accounts Payable Schedule
June 30, 19 –

**Supplementary Exercise (cont.)**

*Green Thumb Garden Centre*

*Bank Reconciliation Statement*

*June 30, 19 —*

| BANK'S RECORD | | COMPANY'S RECORD | |
|---|---|---|---|
| | | | |
| | | | |
| | | | |
| | | | |
| | | | |
| | | | |
| | | | |
| | | | |
| | | | |
| | | | |
| | | | |
| | | | |
| | | | |
| | | | |
| | | | |
| | | | |
| | | | |
| | | | |

# Chapter 14 Payroll Accounting

## ANSWERS TO SECTION 14.1 REVIEW QUESTIONS (text, p. 565)

### Gross Pay

1.
2.
3.
4.
5.
6.
7.
8.
9.
10.
11.
12.
13.
14.

# Chapter 14

Name____________________ Date____________

## ANSWERS TO SECTION 14.1 EXERCISES (text, p. 565)

### Exercise 1, p. 565

| Annual Salary | Payroll Period | Gross Pay per Period |
|---|---|---|
| $ 39 000 | Weekly | |
| | Weekly | $ 800 |
| $ 22 750 | Biweekly | |
| | Biweekly | $ 1 250 |
| $ 36 000 | Semi-monthly | |
| | Semi-monthly | $ 1 800 |
| $ 30 000 | Monthly | |
| | Monthly | $ 3 200 |

### Exercise 2, p. 566

| Payroll Period | Gross Pay |
|---|---|
| a. Weekly | |
| b. Biweekly | |
| c. Semi-monthly | |
| d. Monthly | |

### Exercise 3, p. 566

| Total Hours | Regular Rate | Regular Hours | Overtime Hours | Regular Pay | Overtime Pay | Gross Pay |
|---|---|---|---|---|---|---|
| 46 | $11.50 | | | | | |
| 43 | $14.50 | | | | | |
| 44 $\frac{1}{2}$ | $12.00 | | | | | |
| 54 | $21.00 | | | | | |
| 47 $\frac{1}{4}$ | $13.75 | | | | | |

## ANSWERS TO SECTION 14.1 EXERCISES (cont.)

### Exercise 4, p. 566

| Day | Number of Units Completed | Salary | Piecework Earnings | Gross Pay |
|---|---|---|---|---|
| Monday | 10 | | | |
| Tuesday | 9 | | | |
| Wednesday (1/2) | 5 | | | |
| Thursday | 11 | | | |
| Friday | 10 | | | |
| TOTALS | | | | |

### Exercise 5, p. 567

Time Card

Week Ended July 23 19 --

Social Ins. No. 642 393 438

Name Frank Windsor

| Day | Morning In | Morning Out | Afternoon In | Afternoon Out | Extra In | Extra Out | Total Hours |
|---|---|---|---|---|---|---|---|
| M | 7:58 | 12:01 | 12:58 | 5:01 | | | |
| T | 8:07 | 12:00 | 12:57 | 5:02 | | | |
| W | 7:56 | 12:03 | 12:59 | 5:00 | | | |
| T | 7:59 | 12:02 | 1:01 | 5:03 | | | |
| F | 7:57 | 12:02 | 12:59 | 5:01 | | | |
| S | | | | | | | |
| S | | | | | | | |

| | Hours | Rate | Earnings |
|---|---|---|---|
| Regular Time | | 14.00 | |
| Overtime | | | |
| Gross Pay | | | |

Time Card

Week Ended July 23 19 --

Social Ins. No. 643 461 217

Name Ray Peterson

| Day | Morning In | Morning Out | Afternoon In | Afternoon Out | Extra In | Extra Out | Total Hours |
|---|---|---|---|---|---|---|---|
| M | 7:58 | 12:01 | 1:00 | 5:02 | | | |
| T | 7:59 | 12:00 | 12:58 | 5:01 | 5:59 | 8:55 | |
| W | 7:57 | 12:01 | 12:59 | 5:02 | | | |
| T | 7:56 | 12:01 | 12:58 | 5:03 | | | |
| F | 7:59 | 12:01 | 12:59 | 5:01 | | | |
| S | 7:58 | 12:01 | | | | | |
| S | | | | | | | |

| | Hours | Rate | Earnings |
|---|---|---|---|
| Regular Time | | 12.20 | |
| Overtime | | | |
| Gross Pay | | | |

# Chapter 14

Name____________________ Date____________

## ANSWERS TO SECTION 14.1 EXERCISES (cont.)

**Exercise 6, p. 568**

| Salesperson | Sales for Month | Salary | Commission | Gross Earnings |
|---|---|---|---|---|
| Mary Hunt | $90 000 | | | |
| Anna Mocha | $122 000 | | | |
| Bob Rennie | $75 000 | | | |
| Fay Savard | $316 000 | | | |
| Paul Thors | $50 000 | | | |
| Gloria Unich | $70 000 | | | |
| Gladys Wilson | $26 000 | | | |

## ANSWERS TO SECTION 14.2 REVIEW QUESTIONS (text, p. 587)

### Payroll Deductions and Net Pay

1. ____________________
2. ____________________
3. ____________________
4. ____________________
5. ____________________
6. ____________________
7. ____________________
8. ____________________
9. ____________________
10. ____________________
11. ____________________
12. ____________________
13. ____________________
14. ____________________
15. ____________________

## ANSWERS TO SECTION 14.2 REVIEW QUESTIONS (cont.)

16. ______________________

17. ______________________

18. ______________________

19. ______________________

## ANSWERS TO SECTION 14.2 EXERCISES (text, p. 587)

### Exercise 1, p. 587

1.

| Employee | Biweekly Gross Pay | C.P.P. Deduction | U.I. Deduction | R.P.P. (5%) Deduction |
|---|---|---|---|---|
| F. Mazur | $930 | | | |
| C. Koch | $950 | | | |
| P. Parsons | $1 100 | | | |
| G. Vittelli | $1 050 | | | |
| V. Van Del | $1 300 | | | |

2.

### Exercise 2, p. 588

| Net Claim Code | Gross Earnings | | R.P.P. Deduction 6% | | Union Dues | | Taxable Earnings | | Income Tax Deduction | | C.P.P. Deduction | | U.I. Deduction | |
|---|---|---|---|---|---|---|---|---|---|---|---|---|---|---|
| 10 | 1 150 | — | | | 15 | — | | | | | | | | |
| 8 | 1 275 | — | | | 15 | — | | | | | | | | |
| 5 | 1 325 | — | | | 15 | — | | | | | | | | |
| 1 | 1 180 | — | | | 15 | — | | | | | | | | |
| 2 | 1 230 | — | | | 15 | — | | | | | | | | |
| TOTALS | | | | | | | | | | | | | | |

## ANSWERS TO SECTION 14.2 EXERCISES (cont.)

**Exercise 3, p. 588**

Payroll Journal — For the two weeks ended *June 10* 19—

| Employee | Net Claim Code | Earnings | | | Deductions | | | | | | | | | Net Pay |
|---|---|---|---|---|---|---|---|---|---|---|---|---|---|---|
| | | Regular | Extra | Gross | R.P.P. | Union Dues | Income Tax: Taxable Earnings | Income Tax: Tax Deduction | C.P.P. | U.I. | Health Ins. | Group Life | Total Ded'ns | |
| *J. Bell* | 8 | 1 310 — | | 1 310 — | | | | | | | | | | |
| | | | | | | | | | | | | | | |

**Exercise 4, p. 588**

**a.** An amount kept back from an employee's gross pay is known as a ________________.

**b.** The amount of pay remaining after all deductions have been made is known as _______.

**c.** Payroll calculations are summarized in a book known as the ______________.

**d.** Keeping back an amount from an employee's pay is called __________ it.

**e.** Certain payroll deductions are made on behalf of the federal government. The __________ ________ system is used to keep track of all these deductions for all of the citizens of the country.

**f.** The deductions in **e.** above are for ____________________, __________, and ______________ __________.

**g.** To assist employers in making the deductions in **f.** above, the government provides ____________ _____.

**h.** The Canada Pension Plan deduction and the Unemployment Insurance deduction are based on the _________ figure.

**i.** For the Canada Pension Plan, there is a _________ figure after which no further deductions will be made for the year.

**j.** Employers, as well as employees, must __________ to the Canada Pension Plan and Unemployment Insurance funds.

**k.** A payroll made every two weeks is known as a ________ payroll.

**l.** $23.60 is the maximum unemployment insurance deduction for a ____________ payroll period.

**m.** A private pension plan that is approved by the government is known as a _________ pension plan.

**n.** An employee fills out a TD1 form in order to determine the _______________ figure.

**o.** The ______________ number is based on the figure arrived at in **n.** above.

**p.** The deduction for income tax is not based on gross earnings. It is based on (estimated) ________ earnings.

**q.** The figure in **p.** above is found by making deductions from the gross pay figure. These deductions are allowed by _______________.

**r.** Most provinces operate a ____________________.

**s.** The payroll journal is a ________ journal and therefore must be ____________.

 Name________________ Date__________

## ANSWERS TO SECTION 14.2 EXERCISES (cont.)

**Ex. 4 (cont.)**

List of Words and Phrases

| | | |
|---|---|---|
| biweekly | gross pay | registered |
| Canada Pension Plan | health insurance plan | total exemptions |
| columnar | income tax | Revenue Canada |
| contribute | maximum | unemployment insurance |
| cross balanced | net claim code | semi-monthly |
| deduction tables | net pay | witholding |
| payroll deduction | social insurance number | |
| payroll journal | taxable | |

## ANSWERS TO SECTION 14.3 REVIEW QUESTIONS (text, p. 594)
## Recording the Payroll

1. ________________

2. ________________

3. ________________

5. ________________

6. ________________

7. ________________

8. ________________

9. ________________

10. ________________

11. ________________

12. ________________

 Name________________ Date________________

## ANSWERS TO SECTION 14.3 EXERCISES (text, p. 594)

**Exercise 1, p. 594**

GENERAL JOURNAL PAGE________

| DATE 19— | | PARTICULARS | P.R. | DEBIT | CREDIT |
|---|---|---|---|---|---|
| | | | | | |

## ANSWERS TO SECTION 14.3 EXERCISES (cont.)

**Ex. 1 (cont.)**

Bank

Canada Pension Plan Payable

Unemployment Insurance Payable

Registered Pension Plan Payable

Employees' Income Tax Payable

Health Insurance Payable

Union Dues Payable

Group Life Insurance Payable

Payroll Payable

Salaries Expense

Canada Pension Plan Expense

Unemployment Insurance Expense

Registered Pension Plan Expense

Health Insurance Expense

## ANSWERS TO SECTION 14.3 EXERCISES (cont.)

**Ex. 1 (cont.)**

**6.** **a.** ________________
**b.** ________________
**c.** ________________

**d.** ________________

**Exercise 2, p. 595 (Workbook Exercise)**

Examine the following T-accounts and answer the questions below.

**C.P.P. Payable**

| | Debit | Credit |
|---|---|---|
| Feb | | 185.12 |
| | | 185.12 |
| Mar | 370.24 | |
| | | 190.40 |
| | | 190.40 |
| Apr | 380.80 | |

**U.I. Payable**

| | Debit | Credit |
|---|---|---|
| Feb | | 265.35 |
| | | 371.49 |
| Mar | 636.84 | |
| | | 268.20 |
| | | 375.48 |
| Apr | 643.68 | |

**Empls' Inc. Tax Payable**

| | Debit | Credit |
|---|---|---|
| Feb | | 502.36 |
| Mar | 502.36 | |
| | | 525.24 |
| Apr | 525.25 | |

**a.** How is the $371.49 amount in the U.I. Payable account calculated? ________________

**b.** In the C.P.P. Payable account, why does the $185.12 appear twice? ________________

**c.** What is the length of the pay period? ________________

**d.** What amount was remitted to the federal government in March? ________________

**Exercise 3, p. 595**

**1.** ________________

**2.** ________________

**3.** a) ________________
b) ________________
c) ________________
d) ________________

 Name ______________ Date ______________

## ANSWERS TO SECTION 14.3 EXERCISES (cont.)

**Ex. 3 (cont.)**

4. a) ______________________________

   b) ______________________________

   ______________________________

5. ______________________________

## ANSWERS TO SECTION 14.4 REVIEW QUESTIONS (text, p. 598)

**Payment to Employees**

1. ______________________________

2. ______________________________

3. ______________________________

4. ______________________________

5. ______________________________

6. ______________________________

 Name________________ Date________

## ANSWERS TO SECTION 14.4 EXERCISES (text, p. 598)

**Exercise 1, p. 598 (Workbook Exercise)**

**Shown here is a partial payroll journal for United Wholesale. Prepare the currency requisition form for this payroll.**

PAYROLL JOURNAL

| Employee | | Net Pay |
|---|---|---|
| Anderson M. | | $ 865.56 |
| Chian N. | | 1 256.12 |
| Gerow J. | | 1 002.50 |
| Hills A. | | 852.02 |
| Larocque B. | | 748.96 |
| McComber J. | | 1 158.21 |
| Ruf L. | | 658.87 |
| Spenser M. | | 876.89 |
| Valela C. | | 945.17 |
| Zubak P. | | 1 247.05 |
| *Total* | | |

PAYROLL CURRENCY REQUISITION PERIOD ENDED *March 20* 19 —

| Employee | Net Pay | $20 | $10 | $5 | $1 | 25¢ | 10¢ | 5¢ | 1¢ |
|---|---|---|---|---|---|---|---|---|---|
| Anderson M. | | | | | | | | | |
| Chian N. | | | | | | | | | |
| Gerow J. | | | | | | | | | |
| Hills A. | | | | | | | | | |
| Larocque B. | | | | | | | | | |
| McComber J. | | | | | | | | | |
| Ruf L. | | | | | | | | | |
| Spenser M. | | | | | | | | | |
| Valela C. | | | | | | | | | |
| Zubak P. | | | | | | | | | |
| | | | | | | | | | |
| | | | | | | | | | |
| No. of bills or coins | | | | | | | | | |
| Dollar value | | | | | | | | | |

## ANSWERS TO SECTION 14.4 EXERCISES (cont.)

**Exercise 2, p. 599**

*Central Supply House*
*Bank Reconciliation Statement*
*March 31, 19 –*

**Exercise 3, p. 600**

1.
2.
3.
4.
5.
6.

## ANSWERS TO SECTION 14.5 REVIEW QUESTIONS (text, p. 603)
### Basic Payroll Records

1.

## ANSWERS TO SECTION 14.5 REVIEW QUESTIONS (cont.)

**2.** ______________

**3.** ______________

**4.** ______________

**5.** ______________

**6.** ______________

**7.** ______________

**8.** ______________

## ANSWERS TO SECTION 14.5 EXERCISES (text, p. 604)

**Exercise 1, p. 604**

**1.** a) ______________

b) ______________

c) ______________

d) ______________

e) ______________

 Name ____________ Date ____________

## ANSWERS TO SECTION 14.5 EXERCISES (cont.)

**Ex. 1 (cont.)**

**2.** ____________

**3.** ____________

**Exercise 2, p. 604**

**1.** Box C ____________
Box D ____________
Box E ____________
Box F ____________
Box G ____________

**2.** ____________

 Name________________________ Date________________

## ANSWERS TO CHAPTER 14 EXERCISES (text, p. 606)

### USING YOUR KNOWLEDGE

**Exercise 1, p. 606**

PAYROLL JOURNAL

For the two weeks ended __________ 19 —

| Employee | Net Claim Code | Earnings | | | Deductions | | | | | | | | | | Net Pay |
|---|---|---|---|---|---|---|---|---|---|---|---|---|---|---|---|
| | | Regular | Extra | Gross | R.P.P. | Union Dues | Income Tax | | C.P.P. | U.I. | Health Ins. | Group Life | | Total Ded'ns | |
| | | | | | | | Taxable Earnings | Tax Deduction | | | | | | | |
| | | | | | | | | | | | | | | | |
| | | | | | | | | | | | | | | | |
| | | | | | | | | | | | | | | | |
| | | | | | | | | | | | | | | | |
| | | | | | | | | | | | | | | | |
| | | | | | | | | | | | | | | | |
| | | | | | | | | | | | | | | | |
| | | | | | | | | | | | | | | | |
| | | | | | | | | | | | | | | | |
| | | | | | | | | | | | | | | | |
| | | | | | | | | | | | | | | | |
| | | | | | | | | | | | | | | | |
| | | | | | | | | | | | | | | | |

 Name ______________ Date ______________

## ANSWERS TO CHAPTER 14 EXERCISES (cont.)

**Ex. 1 (cont.)**

### GENERAL JOURNAL

PAGE ______

| DATE 19— | | PARTICULARS | P.R. | DEBIT | CREDIT |
|---|---|---|---|---|---|
| | | | | | |

## ANSWERS TO CHAPTER 14 EXERCISES (cont.)

### Exercise 2, p. 606 (Workbook Exercise)

1. Prepare the payroll journal from the data given below for the two weeks ending September 14, 19 –. Use rates and rules as given in the text if not stated otherwise.

A.

| Employee | Net Claim Code | Biweekly Salary | Health Insurance Status | Life Insurance Coverage |
|---|---|---|---|---|
| Chursa S. | 4 | $1 100.00 | Married | $100 000 |
| Fillion E. | 8 | $1 200.00 | Married | $100 000 |
| Hubie E. | 7 | $1 050.00 | Married | $100 000 |
| Pitt R. | 2 | $1 180.00 | Single | $20 000 |
| Rybar R. | 1 | $1 210.00 | Single | $10 000 |
| Sitch G. | 6 | $1 100.00 | Married | $75 000 |
| Tabor M. | 3 | $1 040.00 | Single | $50 000 |

B. Each employee is enrolled in the registered pension plan with contributions set at six percent of the gross pay. The employer matches the employees' contributions.

C. There is no union.

D. The employer pays one-half of health insurance and life insurance.

2. Total the columns of the payroll journal and perform the steps to ensure its accuracy.
3. Journalize the accounting entries to record all aspects of the payroll and to pay the employees by means of one cheque to the payroll bank account.

## ANSWERS TO CHAPTER 14 EXERCISES (cont.)

**Ex. 2 (cont.)**

PAYROLL JOURNAL

For the two weeks ended 19—

| Employee | Net Claim Code | Earnings | | | Deductions | | | | | | | | | | Net Pay |
|---|---|---|---|---|---|---|---|---|---|---|---|---|---|---|---|
| | | Regular | Extra | Gross | R.P.P. | Union Dues | Income Tax: Taxable Earnings | Income Tax: Tax Deduction | C.P.P. | U.I. | Health Ins. | Group Life | Total Ded'ns | | |
| | | | | | | | | | | | | | | | |
| | | | | | | | | | | | | | | | |
| | | | | | | | | | | | | | | | |
| | | | | | | | | | | | | | | | |
| | | | | | | | | | | | | | | | |
| | | | | | | | | | | | | | | | |
| | | | | | | | | | | | | | | | |
| | | | | | | | | | | | | | | | |
| | | | | | | | | | | | | | | | |
| | | | | | | | | | | | | | | | |
| | | | | | | | | | | | | | | | |
| | | | | | | | | | | | | | | | |
| | | | | | | | | | | | | | | | |

## ANSWERS TO CHAPTER 14 EXERCISES (cont.)

**Ex. 2 (cont.)**

3.

### GENERAL JOURNAL

PAGE__________

| DATE 19— | | PARTICULARS | P.R. | DEBIT | CREDIT |
|---|---|---|---|---|---|
| | | | | | |

## ANSWERS TO CHAPTER 14 EXERCISES (cont.)

**Exercise 3, p. 606**

1.

PAYROLL JOURNAL

For the two weeks ended ____________ 19—

| Employee | Net Claim Code | Earnings | | | Deductions | | | | | | | | | | Net Pay |
|---|---|---|---|---|---|---|---|---|---|---|---|---|---|---|---|
| | | Regular | Extra | Gross | R.P.P. | Union Dues | Income Tax | | C.P.P. | U.I. | Health Ins. | Group Life | | Total Ded'ns | |
| | | | | | | | Taxable Earnings | Tax Deduction | | | | | | | |
| | | | | | | | | | | | | | | | |
| | | | | | | | | | | | | | | | |
| | | | | | | | | | | | | | | | |
| | | | | | | | | | | | | | | | |
| | | | | | | | | | | | | | | | |
| | | | | | | | | | | | | | | | |
| | | | | | | | | | | | | | | | |
| | | | | | | | | | | | | | | | |
| | | | | | | | | | | | | | | | |
| | | | | | | | | | | | | | | | |
| | | | | | | | | | | | | | | | |
| | | | | | | | | | | | | | | | |
| | | | | | | | | | | | | | | | |

## ANSWERS TO CHAPTER 14 EXERCISES (cont.)

**Ex. 3 (cont.)**

**2., 3.**

### GENERAL JOURNAL

PAGE____________

| DATE 19— | | PARTICULARS | P.R. | DEBIT | CREDIT |
|---|---|---|---|---|---|
| | | | | | |
| | | | | | |
| | | | | | |
| | | | | | |
| | | | | | |
| | | | | | |
| | | | | | |
| | | | | | |
| | | | | | |
| | | | | | |
| | | | | | |
| | | | | | |
| | | | | | |
| | | | | | |
| | | | | | |
| | | | | | |
| | | | | | |
| | | | | | |
| | | | | | |
| | | | | | |
| | | | | | |
| | | | | | |
| | | | | | |
| | | | | | |
| | | | | | |
| | | | | | |
| | | | | | |
| | | | | | |
| | | | | | |
| | | | | | |
| | | | | | |
| | | | | | |
| | | | | | |

## ANSWERS TO CHAPTER 14 EXERCISES (cont.)

### COMPREHENSIVE EXERCISES

**Exercise 4, p. 607**

**1.**

**2.**

**3.**

**4.**

**5.**

**6.**

**7.**

**8.**

**Exercise 5, p. 608**

**1.**

Bank

C.P.P. Payable

U.I. Payable

## ANSWERS TO CHAPTER 14 EXERCISES (cont.)

**Ex. 5 (cont.)**

R.P.P. Payable

Empls' Inc. Tax Pay'l

Health Insurance Pay'l

Union Dues Payable

Payroll Payable

Wages Expense

C.P.P. Expense

U.I. Expense

R.P.P. Expense

Health Insce. Expense

**2.** *Expenses* *Cash Paid Out*

 Name ______________ Date ______________

## ANSWERS TO CHAPTER 14 EXERCISES (cont.)

### FOR FURTHER THOUGHT

**Exercise 6, p. 609**

1. ______________
2. ______________
3. ______________
4. ______________
5. ______________
6. ______________
7. ______________
8. ______________
9. ______________
10. ______________
11. ______________
12. ______________

## CASE STUDIES (text, p. 610)

**Case 1** *Comparing Wage Increases*, p. 610

1. ______________
2. ______________

# Chapter 14

Name________________________ Date________________

## CASE STUDIES (cont.)

**Case 2** *Wage Increase — How Much Can Be Offered?*, p. 611

**1.**

**2.**

**3.**

**4.**

**Case 3** *Dummy Employees on the Payroll*, p. 611

**Case 4** *A Profit-Sharing Proposal*, p. 612

**1.**

**2.**

# Chapter 14

Name ____________________ Date ________________

## CASE STUDIES (cont.)

### Case 4 (cont.)

3\.

4\.

5\.

6\.

7\.

8\.

## CASE STUDIES (cont.)

### Case 4 (cont.)

**9.** ____________________

**10.** ____________________

### Case 5 *Employee's Wages — How Much?*, p. 614

**1.** ____________________

**2.** ____________________

**3.** ____________________

**4.** ____________________

**5.** ____________________

# Chapter 14

Name ______________________ Date ______________

## CAREER Thu Vinh Lan/Senior Payroll Supervisor

### ANSWERS TO DISCUSSION QUESTIONS (text, p. 617)

1. ______________________

2. ______________________

3. ______________________

4. ______________________

5. ______________________

# Chapter 15 End-of-Period Accounting

## ANSWERS TO SECTION 15.1 REVIEW QUESTIONS (text, p. 620)

### Accountability

1. ______

2. ______

3. ______

4. ______

5. ______

6. ______

7. ______

8. ______

9. ______

10. ______

11. ______

12. ______

13. ______

14. ______

15. ______

# Chapter 15

Name ______________________ Date ____________

## ANSWERS TO SECTION 15.1 EXERCISE (text, p. 621)

**Exercise 1, p. 621**

1. ______
2. ______
3. ______
4. ______
5. ______
6. ______
7. ______
8. ______
9. ______
10. ______
11. ______
12. ______

## ANSWERS TO SECTION 15.2 REVIEW QUESTIONS (text, p. 628)

### Adjusting for Depreciation

1. ______
2. ______
3. ______
4. ______
5. ______
6. ______
7. ______

## ANSWERS TO SECTION 15.2 REVIEW QUESTIONS (cont.)

8. ____________________

9. ____________________

10. ____________________

11. ____________________

## ANSWERS TO SECTION 15.2 EXERCISES (text, p. 629)

### Exercise 1, p. 629

For each of the following situations divide up the total expense among the proper fiscal periods. Assume a company that commenced business on January 1, 19–1 and has a fiscal year-end of December 31.

1. A truck was purchased on January 1, 19–1 for $18 000. It was expected to last for five full years at the end of which it would have a trade-in value of $3 000. Use the straight-line method of depreciation.

| 19–1 | 19–2 | 19–3 | 19–4 | 19–5 |
|---|---|---|---|---|
| | | | | |

2. A used vechicle was bought on November 1, 19–1 for $5 800. It was expected to last for four full years at the end of which it would have a resale value of $1 000. Use the straight-line method of depreciation.

| 19–1 | 19–2 | 19–3 | 19–4 | 19–5 |
|---|---|---|---|---|
| | | | | |

3. A building was purchased on May 1, 19–2 for the sum of $113 000. It was expected to last for 25 years at which time it would have a resale value of $5 000. Use the straight-line method of depreciation.

| 19–1 | 19–2 | 19–3 | 19–4 | 19–5 |
|---|---|---|---|---|
| | | | | |

Name________________________ Date______________

## ANSWERS TO SECTION 15.2 EXERCISES (cont.)

**Ex. 1 (cont.)**

4. A new machine was bought on January 1, 19–1 for $54 000. It is depreciated using the declining-balance method at the rate of 20 per cent.

| 19–1 | 19–2 | 19–3 | 19–4 | 19–5 |
|---|---|---|---|---|
| | | | | |

5. A new building was bought on July 1, 19–1 for $282 000. It is depreciated using the declining-balance method at the rate of 5 per cent.

| 19–1 | 19–2 | 19–3 | 19–4 | 19–5 |
|---|---|---|---|---|
| | | | | |

**Exercise 2, p. 630**

1.

| Year | Straight-line Depreciation | |
|---|---|---|
| | Depreciation | Balance |
| | | |
| | | |
| | | |
| | | |
| | | |
| | | |
| | | |

2.

| Year | Declining-balance Depreciation | |
|---|---|---|
| | Depreciation | Balance |
| | | |
| | | |
| | | |
| | | |
| | | |
| | | |
| | | |
| | | |

## ANSWERS TO SECTION 15.2 EXERCISES (cont.)

**Exercise 3, p. 630**

**The general ledger of Salk Company at the end of its annual fiscal period appears below.**

1. **Using the additional information that is provided, record the year-end adjusting entries directly in the T-accounts.**
2. **Prepare an adjusted trial balance.**

**1.**

| Bank | |
|---|---|
| 400 | |

| Accounts Rec'l | |
|---|---|
| 8 285 | |

| Supplies | |
|---|---|
| 1 900 | |

| Prepaid Insurance | |
|---|---|
| 1 800 | |

| Land | |
|---|---|
| 50 000 | |

| Buildings | |
|---|---|
| 70 000 | |

| Accum. Deprec. Bldgs. | |
|---|---|
| | 6 750 |

| Equipment | |
|---|---|
| 96 500 | |

| Accum. Deprec. Equip. | |
|---|---|
| | 24 000 |

| Accounts Payable | |
|---|---|
| | 3 200 |

| J. Salk, Capital | |
|---|---|
| | 144 985 |

| J. Salk, Drawings | |
|---|---|
| 30 000 | |

| Revenue | |
|---|---|
| | 140 700 |

| Bank Charges | |
|---|---|
| 450 | |

| Delivery Expense | |
|---|---|
| 1 500 | |

## ANSWERS TO SECTION 15.2 EXERCISES (cont.)

**Ex. 3 (cont.)**

| Light and Heat | |
|---|---|
| 1 300 | |

| Miscellaneous Expense | |
|---|---|
| 490 | |

| Telephone Expense | |
|---|---|
| 390 | |

| Wages Expense | |
|---|---|
| 56 620 | |

| Supplies Used | |
|---|---|
| | |

| Insurance Expense | |
|---|---|
| | |

| Deprec. Buildings | |
|---|---|
| | |

| Deprec. Equipment | |
|---|---|
| | |

**Additional Information**

1. Inventory of supplies at the year-end is $850.
2. Unexpired insurance at the year-end is $625.
3. Depreciation is calculated on a straight-line basis. The building is expected to last 40 years at which time it will be worth $25 000. The equipment is expected to last 15 years after which it will be worth $6 500.

## ANSWERS TO SECTION 15.2 EXERCISES (cont.)

**Ex. 3 (cont.)**

2. Salk Company

Post-Adjustments Trial Balance

## ANSWERS TO SECTION 15.2 EXERCISES (cont.)

**Exercise 4, p. 631 (Workbook Exercise)**

Shown below are the ledger accounts of Sentry Enterprises immediately before making the adjusting entries at the end of an annual fiscal period.

1. Using the additional information that is provided, record the required adjusting entries directly in the T-accounts.
2. Prepare an adjusted trial balance.

1.

| Bank | |
|---|---|
| 1 300 | |

| Accounts Rec'l | |
|---|---|
| 23 500 | |

| Supplies | |
|---|---|
| 2 500 | |

| Prepaid Insce. | |
|---|---|
| 2 400 | |

| Truck | |
|---|---|
| 18 000 | |

| Accum. Depr. Truck | |
|---|---|
| | 5 400 |

| Accounts Pay'l | |
|---|---|
| | 1 350 |

| Kay Dixon, Capital | |
|---|---|
| | 38 802 |

| K. Dixon, Drawings | |
|---|---|
| 10 000 | |

| Revenue | |
|---|---|
| | 39 000 |

| Advertising | |
|---|---|
| 1 585 | |

| Bank Charges | |
|---|---|
| 524 | |

| Gas and Oil | |
|---|---|
| 4 758 | |

| Light and Heat | |
|---|---|
| 4 800 | |

| Miscell. Exp. | |
|---|---|
| 985 | |

 Name__________ Date__________

## ANSWERS TO SECTION 15.2 EXERCISES (cont.)

**Ex. 4 (cont.)**

**1. (cont.)**

| Rent | |
|---|---|
| 12 000 | |

| Telephone | |
|---|---|
| 2 200 | |

| Deprec. Truck | |
|---|---|
| | |

| Insurance Exp. | |
|---|---|
| | |

| Supplies Exp. | |
|---|---|
| | |

**Additional Information**

1. The supplies on hand at the year-end amounted to $875.
2. The unexpired insurance at the year-end amounted to $1 100.
3. Depreciation on the truck is calculated on a straight-line basis. The truck is expected to last for six years at the end of which time it will have a value of $900.

 Name________________ Date__________

## ANSWERS TO SECTION 15.2 EXERCISES (cont.)

**Ex. 4 (cont.)**

2. Sentry Enterprises

Post-Adjustments Trial Balance

– date –

Name______________________ Date______________

## ANSWERS TO SECTION 15.2 EXERCISES (cont.)

### Exercise 5, p. 631

**The following work sheet contains a number of errors. Locate the errors, correct them, and balance the work sheet.**

Pinnacle Company — Work Sheet — Year Ended December *31, 19–*

| ACCOUNTS | TRIAL BALANCE DR | TRIAL BALANCE CR | ADJUSTMENTS DR | ADJUSTMENTS CR | INCOME STATEMENT DR | INCOME STATEMENT CR | BALANCE SHEET DR | BALANCE SHEET CR |
|---|---|---|---|---|---|---|---|---|
| Bank | 3 170 — | | | | | | | |
| Accs. Receivable | 19 473 — | | | | | | | |
| Supplies | 1 850 — | | | 1 200 — | | | 1 850 — | |
| Prepaid Insurance | 4 795 — | | | 3 130 — | | | 7 925 — | |
| Land | 70 000 — | | | | | | | |
| Building | 90 750 — | | | | | | 90 750 — | |
| Accum. Depr. Bldg. | | 12 943 22 | | 3 890 34 | | | | 16 838 56 |
| Office Equipment | 17 350 — | | | | | | 17 350 — | |
| Accum. Depr. Off. Equ. | | 8 466 80 | | 1 776 64 | | | | 10 243 44 |
| Automotive Equip. | 38 429 50 | | | | | | 38 492 50 | |
| Accum. Depr. Auto. Equ. | | 25 248 18 | | 3 954 40 | | | | 3 954 40 |
| Accounts Payable | | 7 216 10 | | 362 — | | | | 7 216 10 |
| Bank Loan | | 15 000 — | | | | 15 000 — | | |
| Mortgage Payable | | 100 000 — | | | | 100 000 — | | |
| S. Bloom, Capital | | 62 483 40 | | | | | | 62 483 40 |
| S. Bloom, Drawings | 25 000 — | | | | | 25 000 — | | |
| Sales | | 99 374 10 | | | | 99 374 10 | | |
| Bank Charges | 1 640 30 | | | | 1 640 — | | | |
| Car Expenses | 7 316 50 | | 157 — | | 7 473 50 | | | |
| Light, Heat, Water | 6 017 — | | | | 6 017 — | | | |
| Miscellaneous Exp. | 1 536 — | | 95 — | | 1 631 — | | | |
| Property Taxes | 2 250 — | | | | 2 250 — | | | |
| Telephone | 1 847 — | | 110 — | | 1 957 — | | | |
| Wages | 39 307 50 | | | | 39 307 50 | | | |
| | 330 731 80 | 330 731 80 | | | | | | |
| Supplies Used | | | 1 200 — | | | | | |
| Insurance Exp. | | | 3 130 — | | | | | |
| Depr. Off. Equip. | | | 1 776 64 | | | | | |
| Depr. Auto. Equip. | | | 3 954 40 | | | | | |
| | | | | | | | | |
| | | | | | 58 672 — | 239 374 10 | 156 367 50 | 100 730 90 |
| | | | | | 180 702 10 | | | 155 636 60 |
| | | | | | 239 374 10 | 239 374 10 | 156 367 50 | 156 367 50 |

Name________________ Date________________

## ANSWERS TO SECTION 15.2 EXERCISES (cont.)

**Exercise 6, p. 632**

*Karen Denby, Real Estate* — *Work Sheet* — *Year Ended September 30, 19–4*

| ACCOUNTS | TRIAL BALANCE | | ADJUSTMENTS | | INCOME STATEMENT | | BALANCE SHEET | |
|---|---|---|---|---|---|---|---|---|
| | DR | CR | DR | CR | DR | CR | DR | CR |
| Bank | 3 800 — | | | | | | | |
| Accounts Receivable | 10 000 — | | | | | | | |
| Supplies | 500 — | | | | | | | |
| Prepaid Insurance | 1 000 — | | | | | | | |
| Prepaid Licences | 400 — | | | | | | | |
| Land | 50 000 — | | | | | | | |
| Building | 70 000 — | | | | | | | |
| Acc. Depr. Building | | 5 600 — | | | | | | |
| Furniture and Equipment | 15 000 — | | | | | | | |
| Acc. Depr. Furn. and Equip. | | 4 000 — | | | | | | |
| Automotive Equipment | 17 000 — | | | | | | | |
| Acc. Depr. Auto. Equip. | | 6 300 — | | | | | | |
| Accounts Payable | | 400 — | | | | | | |
| Bank Loan | | 100 000 — | | | | | | |
| Karen Denby, Capital | | 40 000 — | | | | | | |
| Karen Denby, Drawings | 30 000 — | | | | | | | |
| Commissions Revenue | | 96 600 — | | | | | | |
| Advertising Expense | 4 700 — | | | | | | | |
| Bank Charges | 8 600 — | | | | | | | |
| | | | | | | | | |
| | | | | | | | | |

Name____________________ Date________________

## ANSWERS TO SECTION 15.2 EXERCISES (cont.)

**Ex. 6 (cont.)**

| Account | Debit | Credit |
|---|---|---|
| Car Expenses | 8 000 — | |
| Commissions Expense | 18 000 — | |
| Light and Heat Expense | 2 200 — | |
| Miscellaneous Expense | 200 — | |
| Postage Expense | 600 — | |
| Telephone Expense | 900 — | |
| Wages Expense | 12 000 — | |
| | 252 900 — | 252 900 — |

Name____________________ Date________________

## ANSWERS TO SECTION 15.2 EXERCISES (cont.)

**Exercise 7, p. 633**

*Tom's Plastering* *Work Sheet* *Year Ended October 31, 19–1*

| ACCOUNTS | TRIAL BALANCE | | ADJUSTMENTS | | INCOME STATEMENT | | BALANCE SHEET | |
|---|---|---|---|---|---|---|---|---|
| | DR | CR | DR | CR | DR | CR | DR | CR |
| Bank | 1412 01 | | | | | | | |
| Accounts Receivable | 8025 — | | | | | | | |
| Supplies | 1416 70 | | | | | | | |
| Small Tools | 1903 — | | | | | | | |
| Prepaid Insurance | 2107 80 | | | | | | | |
| Equipment | 9500 — | | | | | | | |
| Acc. Depr. Equip. | | 3200 — | | | | | | |
| Truck | 19 500 — | | | | | | | |
| Acc. Depr. Truck | | 8000 — | | | | | | |
| Accounts Payable | | 2407 35 | | | | | | |
| Bank Loan | | 10 000 — | | | | | | |
| Tom Michaud, Capital | | 18 212 28 | | | | | | |
| Tom Michaud, Drawings | 35 534 — | | | | | | | |
| Revenue | | 120 365 — | | | | | | |
| Bank Interest and Charges | 1325 15 | | | | | | | |
| Materials Used | 25 369 20 | | | | | | | |
| Miscellaneous Expense | 756 32 | | | | | | | |
| Rent Expense | 6000 — | | | | | | | |
| Telephone Expense | 864 32 | | | | | | | |

## ANSWERS TO SECTION 15.2 EXERCISES (cont.)

**Ex. 7 (cont.)**

| Account Title | Debit | Credit |
|---|---|---|
| Truck Expenses | 8 3 2 5 40 | |
| Utilities Expense | 4 5 6 3 26 | |
| Wages Expense | 35 5 8 2 47 | |
| | 162 1 8 4 63 | 162 1 8 4 63 |

## ANSWERS TO SECTION 15.2 EXERCISES (cont.)

**Ex. 7 (cont.)**

## ANSWERS TO SECTION 15.2 EXERCISES (cont.)

**Ex. 7 (cont.)**

# Chapter 15

Name________________ Date________

## ANSWERS TO SECTION 15.3 REVIEW QUESTIONS (text, p. 639)

### Adjusting for Doubtful Accounts

1. ____
2. ____
3. ____
4. ____
5. ____
6. ____
7. ____
8. ____
9. ____
10. ____
11. ____
12. ____
13. ____
14. ____
16. ____
17. ____
18. ____

# Chapter 15

Name ______________________ Date ______________

## ANSWERS TO SECTION 15.3 EXERCISES (text, p. 639)

### Exercise 1, p. 639

1. No matter how carefully the customers' __________ are checked out, there are always some customers who cannot or do not pay.
2. A customer's account is first seen as doubtful if it becomes ______.
3. The ______________ requires that any losses from doubtful accounts be shown as expense in the same period as the sales to which they are related.
4. The ____________________ requires that doubtful accounts not be included in the real value of accounts receivable shown on the balance sheet.
5. An ___________ is a breakdown of customers' accounts showing how long the balances have been unpaid.
6. The Allowance for Doubtful Debts account is a ______ account.
7. Because an account is ______ is a good reason for trying harder to collect it.
8. As long as there is hope of collecting the account, it is kept in the ____________.
9. The adjustment for doubtful debts always involves a ______ to the Allowance account.
10. On the balance sheet the allowance for doubtful debts is deducted from the accounts receivable to show their ______________.
11. A doubtful account becomes a _______ when there is no longer any chance of collecting it.
12. The Allowance account is ______ whenever an account is written off.
13. If the accounts written off were for ___ than the (previous) aging schedule figure, the Allowance account will end up with a credit balance.
14. If the accounts written off were for ____ than the (previous) aging schedule figure, the Allowance account will end up with a debit balance.
15. When a bad debt is recovered, the write-off must be ______.

## ANSWERS TO SECTION 15.3 EXERCISES (cont.)

**Exercise 2, p. 640 (Workbook Exercise)**

Complete the following schedule by filling in the blanks with the correct figures.

| No. | Allowance account balance before adjustment | Allowance figure per new aging schedule | Amount of adjustment |
|---|---|---|---|
| 1. | $27.50 Cr | $300.00 | |
| 2. | $25.00 Dr | $350.00 | |
| 3. | $20.00 Cr | | $400.00 |
| 4. | $35.00 Dr | | $750.00 |
| 5. | | $720.00 | $780.00 |
| 6. | | $290.00 | $250.00 |
| 7. | $55.00 Dr | $922.00 | |
| 8. | $38.00 Cr | $620.00 | |
| 9. | $75.00 Cr | | $850.00 |
| 10. | $50.00 Dr | | $540.00 |

## ANSWERS TO SECTION 15.3 EXERCISES (cont.)

**Exercise 3, p. 640 (Workbook Exercises)**

Complete each of the following simplified work sheets using the additional information given.

**a.**

Quality Company Work Sheet Year Ended Dec. 31, 19–4

| Accounts | Trial Balance | | Adjustments | | Income Statement | | Balance Sheet | |
|---|---|---|---|---|---|---|---|---|
| | Dr | Cr | Dr | Cr | Dr | Cr | Dr | Cr |
| Bank | 120 | | | | | | | |
| Accounts Receivable | 9 000 | | | | | | | |
| Allow Doubtful Dts. | | 100 | | | | | | |
| Accounts Payable | | 4 250 | | | | | | |
| J. Hui, Capital | | 2 770 | | | | | | |
| J. Hui, Drawings | 10 000 | | | | | | | |
| Revenue | | 25 000 | | | | | | |
| Light and Heat | 2 000 | | | | | | | |
| Miscellaneous Exp. | 1 000 | | | | | | | |
| Wages | 10 000 | | | | | | | |
| | 32 120 | 32 120 | | | | | | |
| | | | | | | | | |
| | | | | | | | | |
| | | | | | | | | |
| | | | | | | | | |
| | | | | | | | | |
| | | | | | | | | |

**Additional Information**

The aging schedule as of December 31, 19–4 showed doubtful accounts totaling $740.00.

## ANSWERS TO SECTION 15.3 EXERCISES (cont.)

**Ex. 3 (cont.)**

**b.**

Superior Company | Work Sheet | Year Ended Dec. 31, 19–5

| Accounts | Trial Balance Dr | Trial Balance Cr | Adjustments Dr | Adjustments Cr | Income Statement Dr | Income Statement Cr | Balance Sheet Dr | Balance Sheet Cr |
|---|---|---|---|---|---|---|---|---|
| Bank | 350 | | | | | | | |
| Accounts Receivable | 12 500 | | | | | | | |
| Allow Doubtful Dts. | 20 | | | | | | | |
| Accounts Payable | | 5 100 | | | | | | |
| J. How, Capital | | 5 770 | | | | | | |
| J. How, Drawings | 15 000 | | | | | | | |
| Revenue | | 35 000 | | | | | | |
| Light and Heat | 3 500 | | | | | | | |
| Miscellaneous Exp. | 1 000 | | | | | | | |
| Wages | 13 500 | | | | | | | |
| | 45 870 | 45 870 | | | | | | |

**Additional Information**

The aging schedule as of December 31, 19–5 showed doubtful accounts totaling $1 225.00.

## ANSWERS TO SECTION 15.3 EXERCISES (cont.)

**Exercise 4, p. 640**

### GENERAL JOURNAL

PAGE ______

| DATE 19—6 | | PARTICULARS | P.R. | DEBIT | CREDIT |
|---|---|---|---|---|---|
| | | | | | |

## ANSWERS TO SECTION 15.3 EXERCISES (cont.)

**Ex. 4 (cont.)**

**ACCOUNT** Allowance For Doubtful Accounts **NO.**

| DATE 19—6 | | PARTICULARS | P.R. | DEBIT | CREDIT | D/C | BALANCE |
|---|---|---|---|---|---|---|---|
| Jan | 1 | | | | | C | 850 — |
| | | | | | | | |
| | | | | | | | |
| | | | | | | | |
| | | | | | | | |
| | | | | | | | |

## ANSWERS TO SECTION 15.4 REVIEW QUESTIONS (text, p. 648)

### Adjusting for Accrued Expenses

1. ______
2. ______
3. ______
4. ______
5. ______
6. ______
7. ______
8. ______
9. ______

## ANSWERS TO SECTION 15.4 REVIEW QUESTIONS (cont.)

10. ____________________________________________

## ANSWERS TO SECTION 15.4 EXERCISES (text, p. 648)

### Exercise 1, p. 648 (Workbook Exercise)

For each of the following work sheet situations, work out and enter the adjusting entry for the accrual, and extend the items on the work sheet.

**a.**

Abba Company — Work Sheet — Year Ended Dec. 31, 19–7

| Accounts | Trial Balance | | Adjustments | | Income Statement | | Balance Sheet | |
|---|---|---|---|---|---|---|---|---|
| | Dr | Cr | Dr | Cr | Dr | Cr | Dr | Cr |
| Loan Payable — 9% | | 40 000 | | | | | | |
| | | | | | | | | |
| Interest Expense | 2 700 | | | | | | | |
| | $$$$$$ | $$$$$$ | | | | | | |
| | | | | | | | | |
| | | | | | | | | |

**Additional Information**
The anniversary date of the loan is October 1. Interest is due annually on October 1.

**b.**

Baba Company — Work Sheet — Year Ended Dec. 31, 19–6

| Accounts | Trial Balance | | Adjustments | | Income Statement | | Balance Sheet | |
|---|---|---|---|---|---|---|---|---|
| | Dr | Cr | Dr | Cr | Dr | Cr | Dr | Cr |
| Loan Receivable — 12% | 120 000 | | | | | | | |
| | | | | | | | | |
| Interest Revenue | | 9 600 | | | | | | |
| | $$$$$$ | $$$$$$ | | | | | | |
| | | | | | | | | |
| | | | | | | | | |

**Additional Information**
The anniversary date of the loan is February 28. Interest is due semi-annually on February 28 and August 31.

## ANSWERS TO SECTION 15.4 EXERCISES (cont.)

**Ex. 1 (cont.)**

**c.**

**Abab Company** | **Work Sheet** | **Year Ended Sept. 30, 19–4**

| Accounts | Trial Balance | | Adjustments | | Income Statement | | Balance Sheet | |
|---|---|---|---|---|---|---|---|---|
| | Dr | Cr | Dr | Cr | Dr | Cr | Dr | Cr |
| | | | | | | | | |
| Wages Expense — 12% | 132 654 | | | | | | | |
| | $$$$$$ | $$$$$$ | | | | | | |
| | | | | | | | | |
| | | | | | | | | |
| | | | | | | | | |

**Additional Information**
The payroll for the two-week period ending Friday, October 4 (10 working days) amounted to $5 265.

**d.**

**Baab Company** | **Work Sheet** | **Year Ended March 31, 19–2**

| Accounts | Trial Balance | | Adjustments | | Income Statement | | Balance Sheet | |
|---|---|---|---|---|---|---|---|---|
| | Dr | Cr | Dr | Cr | Dr | Cr | Dr | Cr |
| | | | | | | | | |
| Wages Expense | 452 630 | | | | | | | |
| | $$$$$$ | $$$$$$ | | | | | | |
| | | | | | | | | |
| | | | | | | | | |
| | | | | | | | | |

**Additional Information**
The payroll for the one-week period ending Friday, April 2 (five working days) amounted to $26 305.

## ANSWERS TO SECTION 15.4 EXERCISES (cont.)

**Exercise 2, p. 648**

### GENERAL JOURNAL

PAGE ______

| DATE | | PARTICULARS | P.R. | DEBIT | CREDIT |
|---|---|---|---|---|---|
| 1. | | | | | |
| | | | | | |
| | | | | | |
| 2. | | | | | |
| | | | | | |
| | | | | | |
| 3. | | | | | |
| | | | | | |
| | | | | | |

## ANSWERS TO SECTION 15.4 EXERCISES (cont.)

**Exercise 3, p. 648**

**Morrow Company has a June 30th year-end. Shown below is the work sheet for the year ended June 30, 19–9 with the trial balance figures (simplified) entered.**

**Work out the adjusting entries from the additional information given below, and complete the work sheet. Assume that there are no other adjustments.**

**Morrow Company** **Work Sheet** **Year Ended June 30, 19–9**

| Accounts | Trial Balance | | Adjustments | | Income Statement | | Balance Sheet | |
|---|---|---|---|---|---|---|---|---|
| | Dr | Cr | Dr | Cr | Dr | Cr | Dr | Cr |
| Bank | 5 000 | | | | | | | |
| Loan Receivable — 12% | 100 000 | | | | | | | |
| Other Assets | 300 000 | | | | | | | |
| Liabilities | | 121 000 | | | | | | |
| Morrow, Capital | | 186 000 | | | | | | |
| Morrow, Drawings | 50 000 | | | | | | | |
| Sales | | 300 000 | | | | | | |
| Interest Revenue | | 10 000 | | | | | | |
| Rent Expense | 5 000 | | | | | | | |
| Salaries | 102 000 | | | | | | | |
| Other Expenses | 55 000 | | | | | | | |
| | 617 000 | 617 000 | | | | | | |
| | | | | | | | | |
| | | | | | | | | |
| | | | | | | | | |
| | | | | | | | | |
| | | | | | | | | |
| | | | | | | | | |
| | | | | | | | | |
| | | | | | | | | |
| | | | | | | | | |

**Additional Information**

1. The loan was originally granted on April 30, 19–0. Interest is due annually on April 30.
2. The executives are to receive a salary bonus equal to two per cent of the sales figure.
3. Rent, at the rate of $500 per month, is paid every three months. The next rent payment is due on July 31.

 Name__________ Date__________

## ANSWERS TO SECTION 15.4 EXERCISES (cont.)

### Exercise 4, p. 649 (Workbook Exercise)

Fonda Company has a April 30th year-end. Shown on page 650 is the work sheet for the year ended April 30, 19–7 with the trial balance figures (simplified) entered.

Work out the adjusting entries from the additional information given below, and complete the work sheet. Assume that there are no other adjustments.

Fonda Company — Work Sheet — Year Ended April 30, 19–7

| Accounts | Trial Balance | | Adjustments | | Income Statement | | Balance Sheet | |
|---|---|---|---|---|---|---|---|---|
| | Dr | Cr | Dr | Cr | Dr | Cr | Dr | Cr |
| Bank | 5 000 | | | | | | | |
| Other Assets | 410 000 | | | | | | | |
| Loan Payable — 15% | | 70 000 | | | | | | |
| Other Liabilities | | 152 625 | | | | | | |
| Fonda, Capital | | 169 625 | | | | | | |
| Fonda, Drawings | 50 000 | | | | | | | |
| Sales | | 400 000 | | | | | | |
| Interest Expense | 5 250 | | | | | | | |
| Rent Expense | 8 000 | | | | | | | |
| Salaries Expense | 80 000 | | | | | | | |
| Wages Expense | 140 000 | | | | | | | |
| Other Expenses | 94 000 | | | | | | | |
| | 792 250 | 792 250 | | | | | | |
| | | | | | | | | |
| | | | | | | | | |
| | | | | | | | | |
| | | | | | | | | |
| | | | | | | | | |
| | | | | | | | | |
| | | | | | | | | |
| | | | | | | | | |

### Additional Information

1. The loan anniversary date and interest payment date is October 31.
2. Rent is paid half-yearly on February 28 and August 31 at the rate of $800 per month.
3. The wages for the five working days ended May 1 amounted to $3 000.
4. The executives are to receive a salary bonus equal to three per cent of sales.

## ANSWERS TO SECTION 15.4 EXERCISES (cont.)

**Exercise 5, p. 650**

 Name______________________ Date____________

## ANSWERS TO SECTION 15.4 EXERCISES (cont.)

**Ex. 5 (cont.)**

 Name__________________ Date____________

## ANSWERS TO SECTION 15.5 REVIEW QUESTIONS (text, p. 656)

### Reversing Entries

1.

2.

3.

4.

5.

6.

7.

8.

9.

## ANSWERS TO SECTION 15.5 EXERCISES (text, p. 657)

### Exercise 1, p. 657

1.

| | | | | | | | | | |
|---|---|---|---|---|---|---|---|---|---|
| | | | | | | | | | |
| | | | | | | | | | |
| | | | | | | | | | |
| | | | | | | | | | |
| | | | | | | | | | |

2.

| | | | | | | | | | |
|---|---|---|---|---|---|---|---|---|---|
| | | | | | | | | | |
| | | | | | | | | | |
| | | | | | | | | | |
| | | | | | | | | | |
| | | | | | | | | | |

### Exercise 2, p. 657

1. *Summary of late-arriving invoices.*

 Name________________ Date________________

## ANSWERS TO SECTION 15.5 EXERCISES (cont.)

**Ex. 2 (cont.)**

**1. (cont.)**

GENERAL JOURNAL PAGE ______

| DATE | | PARTICULARS | P.R. | DEBIT | CREDIT |
|---|---|---|---|---|---|
| | | *Adjusting Entry* | | | |
| | | | | | |
| | | | | | |
| | | | | | |
| | | | | | |
| | | | | | |
| | | | | | |
| | | | | | |
| | | | | | |
| | | | | | |
| | | | | | |
| 2. | | *Reversing Entry* | | | |
| | | | | | |
| | | | | | |
| | | | | | |
| | | | | | |
| | | | | | |
| | | | | | |
| | | | | | |
| | | | | | |
| | | | | | |
| | | *Post-Closing Trial Balance* | | | |
| | | *December 31, 19–4* | | | |
| | | | | | |
| | | | | | |
| | | | | | |
| | | | | | |
| | | | | | |
| | | | | | |
| | | | | | |
| | | | | | |

## ANSWERS TO SECTION 15.5 EXERCISES (cont.)

### Exercise 3, p. 658 (Workbook Exercise)

Shown below are the T-account ledger and the work sheet for Kisik Company at the end of the 19–4 fiscal period.

**T-account Ledger**

| Bank | | Other Assets | | Accounts Payable | | Payroll Payable | |
|---|---|---|---|---|---|---|---|
| 1 000 | | 10 000 | | | 1 500 | | |

| Capital | | Drawings | | Revenue | | Expense A | |
|---|---|---|---|---|---|---|---|
| | 7 500 | 5 000 | | | 20 000 | 2 000 | |

| Expense B | | Wages | | Accrued Wages Payable | | Income Summary | |
|---|---|---|---|---|---|---|---|
| 3 000 | | 8 000 | | | | | |

1. Journalize the adjusting entries for late invoices and for accrued payroll.
2. Post the above entries (informally) to the T-accounts.
3. Journalize and post the closing entries.
4. Take off a post-closing trial balance.
5. Act as the invoice-processing department: journalize and post the late invoices in 19–5.
6. Act as the payroll department: journalize and post the first payroll ($1 500) on January 5.
7. Act as the accountant: journalize and post the two reversing entries.
8. Study the accounts to ensure that the expenses have been recorded in their proper accounting period.

Name________________ Date____________

## ANSWERS TO SECTION 15.5 EXERCISES (cont.)

**Ex. 3 (cont.)**

*Kisik Company* — *Work Sheet* — *Year Ended December* 31, 19–4

| ACCOUNTS | TRIAL BALANCE DR | TRIAL BALANCE CR | ADJ. ENTRIES DR | ADJ. ENTRIES CR | INCOME STATEMENT DR | INCOME STATEMENT CR | BALANCE SHEET DR | BALANCE SHEET CR |
|---|---|---|---|---|---|---|---|---|
| Bank | 1000 – | | | | | | 1000 – | |
| Other Assets | 10000 – | | | | | | 10000 – | |
| Accs Payable | | 1500 – | | ① 400 – | | | | 1900 – |
| Capital | | 7500 – | | | | | | 7500 – |
| Drawings | 5000 – | | | | | | 5000 – | |
| Revenue | | 20000 – | | | | 20000 – | | |
| Expense A | 2000 – | | ① 50 – | | 2050 – | | | |
| Expense B | 3000 – | | ① 350 – | | 3350 – | | | |
| Wages | 8000 – | | ② 900 – | | 8900 – | | | |
| | 29000 – | 29000 – | | | | | | |
| Accrued Wages Payable | | | | ② 900 – | | | | 900 – |
| | | | 1300 – | 1300 – | 14300 – | 20000 – | 16000 – | 10300 – |
| Net Income | | | | | 5700 – | | | 5700 – |
| | | | | | 20000 – | 20000 – | 16000 – | 16000 – |

## ANSWERS TO SECTION 15.5 EXERCISES (cont.)

**Ex. 3 (cont.)**

### GENERAL JOURNAL

PAGE ______

| DATE 19—4 | | PARTICULARS | P.R. | DEBIT | CREDIT |
|---|---|---|---|---|---|
| | | | | | |

## ANSWERS TO SECTION 15.5 EXERCISES (cont.)

**Exercise 4, p. 659 (Workbook Exercise)**

Show where each step in the accounting cycle should appear in the chart by entering the number of its location in the circle provided.

**Steps in the Accounting Cycle**

Reversing Entries Journalized and Posted ◯

Performed Daily ◯

Ledger Balanced by Means of a Trial Balance ◯

Post-Closing Trial Balance ◯

Performed by Senior Personnel ◯

Performed Monthly ◯

Accounting Entries Recorded in the Journal ◯

Adjusting Entries Journalized and Posted ◯

Performed by Junior Personnel ◯

Income Statement and Balance Sheet Prepared ◯

Performed at the End of the Fiscal Period ◯

Transactions Occur Source Documents ◯

Closing Entries Journalized and Posted ◯

Journal Entries Posted to the Ledger Accounts ◯

Work Sheet Prepared ◯

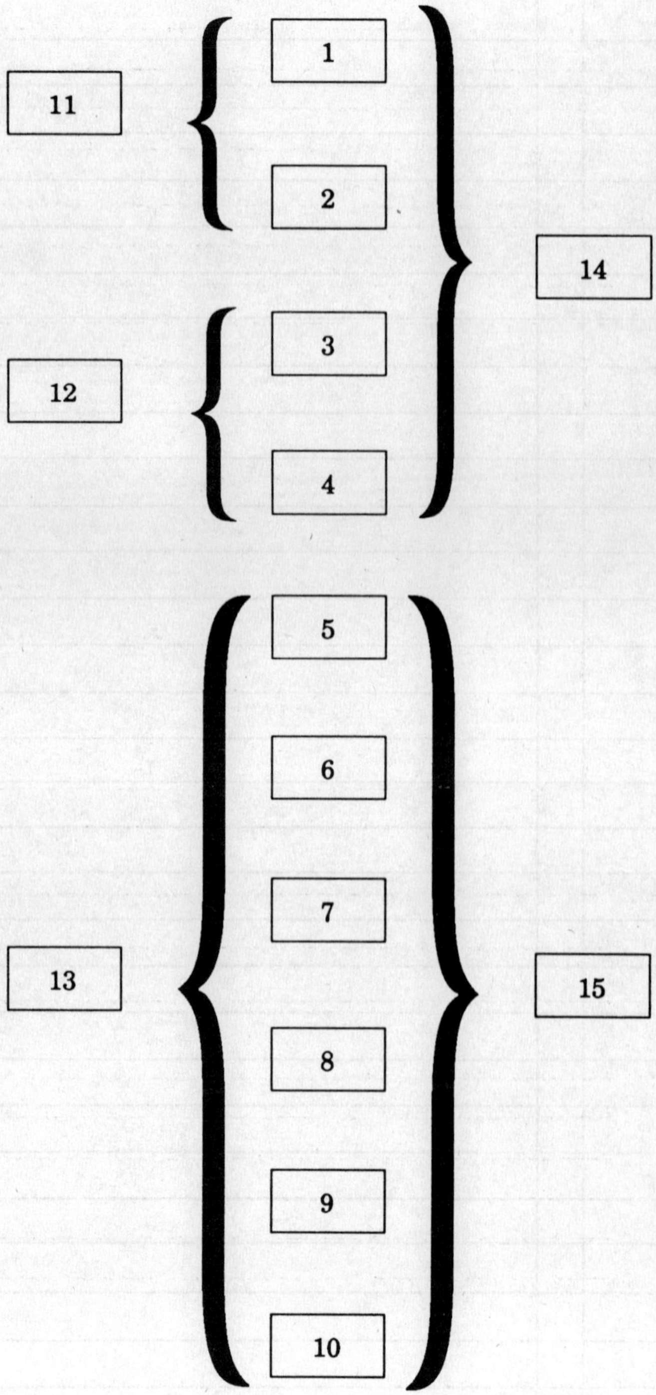

# Chapter 15

Name______________________ Date______________

## ANSWERS TO CHAPTER 15 EXERCISES (text, p. 660)

### USING YOUR KNOWLEDGE

**Exercise 1, p. 660**

**1.** ______________________________

**2.** ______________________________

**3.** ______________________________

**4.** ______________________________

**5.** ______________________________

**6.** ______________________________

**7.** ______________________________

 Name________________ Date__________

## ANSWERS TO CHAPTER 15 EXERCISES (text, p. 660)

**Ex. 1 (cont.)**

**8.**

**9.**

**10.**

**11.**

**12.**

## ANSWERS TO CHAPTER 15 EXERCISES (cont.)

**Exercise 2, p. 661**

| *Year* | *Insurance Expense for Year* | *Value of Prepaid Insurance at Year-end* |
|---|---|---|
| 19 – 1 | | |
| 19 – 2 | | |
| 19 – 3 | | |

**Exercise 3, p. 662**

**a)**

| *Year* | *Straight-line Method* *Depreciation* | *Balance* |
|---|---|---|
| | | |
| | | |
| | | |
| | | |
| | | |
| | | |

**b)**

| *Year* | *Declining-balance Method* *Depreciation* | *Balance* |
|---|---|---|
| | | |
| | | |
| | | |
| | | |
| | | |
| | | |

## ANSWERS TO CHAPTER 15 EXERCISES (cont.)

### Exercise 4, p. 662 (Workbook Exercise)

Anaconda Company began business on January 1, 19–4. The following schedule shows all the expenditures for insurance made by the company in 19–4, 19–5, and 19–6.

1. Complete the last three columns of the schedule.

| Company | Date of Issue | Term | Premium | Unexpired Insurance at | | |
|---|---|---|---|---|---|---|
| | | | | Dec 31/-4 | Dec 31/-5 | Dec 31/-6 |
| Admiral | Mar 1, 19–4 | 1 yr | $576 | | | |
| Municipal | Sep 1, 19–4 | 1 yr | 216 | | | |
| Partners | Jun 1, 19–5 | 2 yrs | 360 | | | |
| Hanover | Aug 1, 19–5 | 1 yr | 396 | | | |
| Municipal | Sep 1, 19–5 | 1 yr | 216 | | | |
| Municipal | Sep 1, 19–6 | 1 yr | 216 | | | |

### Exercise 5, p. 662

1. ________________
2. ________________
3. ________________
4. ________________
5. ________________
6. ________________
7. ________________
8. ________________
9. ________________
10. ________________

## ANSWERS TO CHAPTER 15 EXERCISES (cont.)

### Exercise 6, p. 664

1.

2.

3.

4.

5.

6.

7.

### Exercise 7, p. 665

1.

2.

3.

 Name________________ Date________

## ANSWERS TO CHAPTER 15 EXERCISES (cont.)

**Ex. 7 (cont.)**

4. ____________________

5. ____________________

6. ____________________

7. ____________________

8. ____________________

9. ____________________

10. ____________________

**Exercise 8, p. 667**

1. ____________________

2. ____________________

3. ____________________

# Chapter 15

Name ____________________ Date ____________

## ANSWERS TO CHAPTER 15 EXERCISES (cont.)

### Exercise 9, p. 667

### Exercise 10, p. 667

1. ______________________________
2. ______________________________
3. ______________________________

## ANSWERS TO CHAPTER 15 EXERCISES (cont.)

**Exercise 11, p. 668**

1.

*Marlin Marine*

*Work Sheet*

| ACCOUNTS | TRIAL BALANCE | | ADJUSTMENTS | | INCOME STATEMENT | | BALANCE SHEET | |
|---|---|---|---|---|---|---|---|---|
| | DR | CR | DR | CR | DR | CR | DR | CR |
| Bank | 3 642 09 | | | | | | | |
| Accounts Receivable | 26 319 04 | | | | | | | |
| Allowance for Doubtful Accs. | | 179 15 | | | | | | |
| Merchandise Inventory | 170 209 41 | | | | | | | |
| Supplies | 2 655 — | | | | | | | |
| Prepaid Insurance | 2 956 — | | | | | | | |
| Land | 90 000 — | | | | | | | |
| Buildings | 120 309 — | | | | | | | |
| Accum. Deprec. Buildings | | 17 159 06 | | | | | | |
| General Equipment | 56 237 50 | | | | | | | |
| Accum. Deprec. Gen. Equip. | | 27 443 90 | | | | | | |
| Automotive Equipment | 48 962 11 | | | | | | | |
| Accum. Deprec. Auto. Equip. | | 32 168 11 | | | | | | |
| Accounts Payable | | 39 374 17 | | | | | | |
| Sales Tax Payable | | 2 389 60 | | | | | | |
| Bank Loan | | 148 000 — | | | | | | |
| M. McIvor, Capital | | 242 541 10 | | | | | | |
| M. McIvor, Drawings | 40 000 — | | | | | | | |
| Sales | | 425 931 20 | | | | | | |
| Bank Charges | 18 026 19 | | | | | | | |
| Building Repairs | 3 751 70 | | | | | | | |
| Car and Truck Expense | 26 491 30 | | | | | | | |
| Freight-in | 4 976 21 | | | | | | | |
| Light, Heat, and Water | 2 627 48 | | | | | | | |
| Miscellaneous Expense | 1 924 30 | | | | | | | |

## ANSWERS TO CHAPTER 15 EXERCISES (cont.)

**Ex. 11 (cont.)**

**1. (cont.)**

| | | |
|---|---|---|
| Purchases | 216 3 0 7 06 | |
| Telephone | 2 4 9 7 60 | |
| Wages | 97 2 9 4 30 | |
| | 935 1 8 6 29 | 935 1 8 6 29 |

 Name______________ Date______________

## ANSWERS TO CHAPTER 15 EXERCISES (cont.)

**Ex. 11 (cont.)**

**2.** ______________________________

## ANSWERS TO CHAPTER 15 EXERCISES (cont.)

**Ex. 11 (cont.)**

**2. (cont.)** ______________________________

 Name________________ Date________________

## ANSWERS TO CHAPTER 15 EXERCISES (cont.)

**Ex. 11 (cont.)**

3.

### GENERAL JOURNAL

PAGE ________

| DATE 19—5 | | PARTICULARS | P.R. | DEBIT | CREDIT |
|---|---|---|---|---|---|
| | | | | | |

 Name ________ Date ________

## ANSWERS TO CHAPTER 15 EXERCISES (cont.)

**Ex. 11 (cont.)**

**3. (cont.), 4.**

### GENERAL JOURNAL

PAGE ______

| DATE 19—5 | | PARTICULARS | P.R. | DEBIT | CREDIT |
|---|---|---|---|---|---|
| | | | | | |

## ANSWERS TO CHAPTER 15 EXERCISES (cont.)

### Exercise 12, p. 669 (Workbook Exercise)

Given below is the general ledger trial balance of Asia Importing Company as of December 31, 19–5, the end of a fiscal year.

Asia Importing company
Trial Balance
December 31, 19–5

| | DR | CR |
|---|---|---|
| Petty Cash | 500 00 | |
| Bank | 2 469 25 | |
| Accounts Receivable | 86 319 04 | |
| Allowance for Doubtful Accounts | 124 50 | |
| Merchandise Inventory | 220 759 10 | |
| Supplies | 4 236 52 | |
| Prepaid Insurance | 3 548 00 | |
| Equipment | 36 980 00 | |
| Accumulated Depreciation — Equipment | | 10 660 00 |
| Automobiles | 46 450 00 | |
| Accumulated Depreciation — Automobiles | | 16 180 00 |
| Accounts Payable | | 41 964 75 |
| Sales Tax Payable | | 4 785 00 |
| Bank Loan | | 150 000 00 |
| O. Sakata, Capital | | 112 532 69 |
| O. Sakata, Drawings | 50 000 — | |
| Sales | | 745 655 53 |
| Sales Returns and Allowances | 30 654 80 | |
| Bank Charges and Interest | 15 852 00 | |
| Car Expense | 18 569 20 | |
| Cash Short or Over | 120 00 | |
| Duty | 5 650 25 | |
| Freight-in | 4 896 35 | |
| Light, Heat, and Water | 5 233 50 | |
| Miscellaneous Expense | 1 846 35 | |
| Postage | 847 24 | |
| Purchases | 468 806 57 | |
| Purchases Returns and Allowances | | 28 365 24 |
| Rent | 24 000 00 | |
| Telephone | 3 585 00 | |
| Wages | 78 695 54 | |
| | 1 110 143 21 | 1 110 143 21 |

## ANSWERS TO CHAPTER 15 EXERCISES (cont.)

**Ex. 12 (cont.)**

1. Using the additional information given below, complete the work sheet for the year ended December 31, 19–5.

   **Additional Information**

   a. Purchase invoices received subsequent to the year-end but pertaining to the fiscal period just ended are summarized as follows:

   | | |
   |---|---|
   | Supplies | $496.50 |
   | Freight-in | 1 200.00 |
   | Car Expenses | 450.25 |
   | Miscellaneous Expense | 102.25 |
   | Merchandise for resale | 5 256.32 |

   b. The following four accounts receivable are shown as doubtful on the aging schedule:

   | | |
   |---|---|
   | R. Eriksen | $524.20 |
   | H. Guha | 105.25 |
   | P. Kissel | 325.00 |
   | Morgan & Morgan | $487.56 |

   c. Inventories at December 31, 19-5 are as follows:

   | | |
   |---|---|
   | Merchandise for resale | $215 654.20 |
   | Supplies | 2 848.60 |

   d. Prepaid insurance at December 31 was calculated at $1 417.50.

   e. Depreciation is calculated on a straight-line basis as follows:
      1. Equipment is expected to have a trade-in value of $5 000 and a life of 15 years.
      2. Automotive Equipment is expected to have a trade-in value of $6 000 and a life of five years.

   f. Wages for the two weeks ended Friday, January 8, amounted to $3 026.75. The employees work a five-day week and are paid for New Year's Day, a holiday.

   g. One month's interest on the bank loan is owed as of the year-end. The interest rate is 15 per cent.

2. Prepare the balance sheet and the income statement.
3. Journalize the adjusting and the closing entries.
4. Journalize the reversing entries.

 Name________________ Date________________

## ANSWERS TO CHAPTER 15 EXERCISES (cont.)

**Ex. 12 (cont.)**

**1.**

*Asia Importing Company* — *Work Sheet*

| ACCOUNTS | TRIAL BALANCE DR | TRIAL BALANCE CR | ADJUSTMENTS DR | ADJUSTMENTS CR | INCOME STATEMENT DR | INCOME STATEMENT CR | BALANCE SHEET DR | BALANCE SHEET CR |
|---|---|---|---|---|---|---|---|---|
| Petty Cash | 500 — | | | | | | | |
| Bank | 2 469 25 | | | | | | | |
| Accounts Receivable | 86 319 04 | | | | | | | |
| Allowance for Doubtful Accs. | 124 50 | | | | | | | |
| Merchandise Inventory | 220 759 10 | | | | | | | |
| Supplies | 4 236 52 | | | | | | | |
| Prepaid Insurance | 3 548 — | | | | | | | |
| Equipment | 36 980 — | | | | | | | |
| Accum. Deprec. Equipment | | 10 660 — | | | | | | |
| Automobiles | 46 450 — | | | | | | | |
| Accum. Deprec. Autos | | 16 180 — | | | | | | |
| Accounts Payable | | 41 964 75 | | | | | | |
| Sales Tax Payable | | 4 785 — | | | | | | |
| Bank Loan | | 150 000 — | | | | | | |
| O. Sakata, Capital | | 112 532 69 | | | | | | |
| O. Sakata, Drawings | 50 000 — | | | | | | | |
| Sales | | 745 655 53 | | | | | | |
| Sales Returns & Allowances | 30 654 80 | | | | | | | |
| Bank Charges & Interest | 15 852 — | | | | | | | |
| Car Expense | 18 569 20 | | | | | | | |
| Cash Short or Over | 120 — | | | | | | | |
| Duty | 56 650 25 | | | | | | | |
| Freight-in | 4 896 35 | | | | | | | |
| Light, Heat, & Water | 5 233 50 | | | | | | | |
| Miscellaneous Expense | 1 846 35 | | | | | | | |
| Postage | 847 24 | | | | | | | |
| | | | | | | | | |
| | | | | | | | | |
| | | | | | | | | |

 Name____________________ Date________________

## ANSWERS TO CHAPTER 15 EXERCISES (cont.)

### Ex. 12 (cont.)

**1. (cont.)**

| Account | Debit | Credit |
|---|---|---|
| Purchases | 468 8 0 6 57 | |
| Purchases Returns & Allows. | | 28 3 6 5 24 |
| Rent | 24 0 0 0 — | |
| Telephone | 3 5 8 5 — | |
| Wages | 78 6 9 5 54 | |
| | 1110 1 4 3 21 | 1110 1 4 3 21 |

## ANSWERS TO CHAPTER 15 EXERCISES (cont.)

**Ex. 12 (cont.)**

**2.** ________________________________________

## ANSWERS TO CHAPTER 15 EXERCISES (cont.)

**Ex. 12 (cont.)**

**2. (cont.)**

 Name__________________ Date__________

## ANSWERS TO CHAPTER 15 EXERCISES (cont.)

**Ex. 12 (cont.)**

3.

### GENERAL JOURNAL

PAGE ________

| DATE 19—5 | | PARTICULARS | P.R. | DEBIT | CREDIT |
|---|---|---|---|---|---|

 Name ____________ Date ____________

## ANSWERS TO CHAPTER 15 EXERCISES (cont.)

**Ex. 12 (cont.)**

**3. (cont.), 4.**

### GENERAL JOURNAL

PAGE ______

| DATE 19—5 | | PARTICULARS | P.R. | DEBIT | CREDIT |
|---|---|---|---|---|---|
| | | | | | |

## ANSWERS TO CHAPTER 15 EXERCISES (cont.)

### Exercise 13, p. 669 (Workbook Exercise)

On December 31, 19–4, the end of a fiscal year, the general ledger trial balance of Domino Real Estate is as follows:

DOMINO REAL ESTATE
TRIAL BALANCE
DECEMBER 31, 19–4

| | DR | CR |
|---|---|---|
| Bank | 4 012 25 | |
| Accounts Receivable | 15 650 00 | |
| Allowance for Doubtful Accounts | | 167 00 |
| Investment – 12% Government Bonds | 50 000 00 | |
| Supplies | 2 850 00 | |
| Prepaid Insurance | 2 890 00 | |
| Land | 33 950 00 | |
| Buildings | 42 250 00 | |
| Accumulated Depreciation of Buildings | | 10 750 00 |
| Furniture and Equipment | 13 350 00 | |
| Accumulated Depreciation — Furn. & Equip. | | 4 800 00 |
| Automobiles | 75 000 00 | |
| Accumulated Depreciation — Automobiles | | 30 000 00 |
| Accounts Payable | | 13 356 00 |
| Loan Payable — 6% | | 20 000 00 |
| Mortgage Payable — 12% | | 50 000 00 |
| J. Lamp, Capital | | 67 853 65 |
| J. Lamp, Drawings | 42 000 00 | |
| Commissions Earned | | 153 560 00 |
| Interest Earned | | 5 000 00 |
| Advertising | 8 525 00 | |
| Bank Charges | 325 35 | |
| Building Maintenance | 1 257 25 | |
| Car Expenses | 17 356 80 | |
| Interest Expense — Loan | 900 00 | |
| Interest Expense — Mortgage | | |
| Light, Heat, and Water | 2 856 00 | |
| Miscellaneous Expense | 956 00 | |
| Postage | 1 356 00 | |
| Property Taxes | 1 050 00 | |
| Telephone | 2 596 00 | |
| Wages and Salaries | 31 356 00 | |
| | 355 486 65 | 355 486 65 |

## ANSWERS TO CHAPTER 15 EXERCISES (cont.)

**Ex. 13 (cont.)**

1. Using the additional information given below, complete a work sheet for Domino Real Estate.

**Additional Information**

a. Purchase invoices received in January, 19-5, which pertain to goods or services received in 19-4 are for the following:

| | |
|---|---|
| Building Maintenance | $358.00 |
| Supplies | 185.90 |
| Car Expense | 489.00 |
| Advertising | 500.00 |

b. The allowance for doubtful debts figure was set at $740.00.

c. The supplies counted and valued as of December 31, 19-4, amounted to $750.00.

d. The details of insurance policies in force at December 31, 19-4 are:

| *Company* | *Policy Date* | *Term* | *Premium* |
|---|---|---|---|
| Acme | July 1, 19-4 | 1 year | $240 |
| Inland | August 1, 19-4 | 1 year | 192 |
| Empire | December 1, 19-4 | 2 years | 432 |
| Imperial | December 1, 19-4 | 1 year | 288 |

e. Depreciation is calculated on a straight-line basis. Buildings cost $42 250, are expected to have a useful life of 30 years, and to have a market value of $10 000 at the end of that time. Furniture and equipment cost $13 350, are expected to have a useful life of 15 years, and to have a market value of $1 350 at the end of that time.
Automobiles cost $75 000, are expected to have a useful life of five years, and to have a resale value of $25 000 at the end of that time.

f. The full amount of the mortgage payable is due in 19–9. The interest is payable every December 31. The 19–4 interest was not paid until early in 19–5.

g. The loan payable of $20 000 bears interest at the rate of six per cent per annum. Interest payments of $300 are made at the end of each quarter year. However, the last payment for 19–4 was not made on time.

h. The Government of Canada bonds pay interest every June 30 and December 31. The procedure is to clip the proper interest coupon from the bond and to deposit it in the bank account. This was done promptly at June 30 but not at December 31. Accrued wages at December 31 amounted to $902.32.

2. Prepare a balance sheet and an income statement.

3. Journalize the reversing entries.

Name________________ Date________________

## ANSWERS TO CHAPTER 15 EXERCISES (cont.)

**Ex. 13 (cont.)**

1.

*Domino Real Estate*

*Work Sheet*

| ACCOUNTS | TRIAL BALANCE DR | TRIAL BALANCE CR | ADJUSTMENTS DR | ADJUSTMENTS CR | INCOME STATEMENT DR | INCOME STATEMENT CR | BALANCE SHEET DR | BALANCE SHEET CR |
|---|---|---|---|---|---|---|---|---|
| Bank | 4 012 25 | | | | | | | |
| Accounts Receivable | 15 650 — | | | | | | | |
| Allowance Doubtful Accs | | 167 — | | | | | | |
| Investment 20% Gov't Bonds | 50 000 — | | | | | | | |
| Supplies | 2 850 — | | | | | | | |
| Prepaid Insurance | 2 890 — | | | | | | | |
| Land | 38 950 — | | | | | | | |
| Buildings | 42 250 — | | | | | | | |
| Accum. Depr. Bldgs. | | 10 750 — | | | | | | |
| Furniture & Equipment | 13 350 — | | | | | | | |
| Accum. Depr. Furn. & Equip. | | 4 800 — | | | | | | |
| Automobiles | 75 000 — | | | | | | | |
| Accum. Deprec. Autos | | 30 000 — | | | | | | |
| Accounts Payable | | 13 356 — | | | | | | |
| Loan Payable — 6% | | 20 000 — | | | | | | |
| Mortgage Payable — 12% | | 50 000 — | | | | | | |
| J. Lamp, Capital | | 67 853 65 | | | | | | |
| J. Lamp, Drawings | 42 000 — | | | | | | | |
| Commissions Earned | | 153 560 — | | | | | | |
| Interest Earned | | 5 000 — | | | | | | |
| Advertising | 8 525 — | | | | | | | |
| Bank Charges | 325 35 | | | | | | | |
| Building Maintenance | 1 257 25 | | | | | | | |
| Car Expenses | 17 356 80 | | | | | | | |
| Interest Expense — Loan | 900 — | | | | | | | |
| Interest Exp. — Mortgage | | | | | | | | |

Name______________ Date______________

## ANSWERS TO CHAPTER 15 EXERCISES (cont.)

**Ex. 13 (cont.)**

**1. (cont.)**

| Account | Debit | Credit |
|---|---|---|
| Light, Heat, & Water | 2 856 — | |
| Miscellaneous Expense | 956 — | |
| Postage | 1 356 — | |
| Property Taxes | 1 050 — | |
| Telephone | 2 596 — | |
| Wages & Salaries | 31 356 — | |
| | 355 486 65 | 355 486 65 |

 Name_____________________ Date______________

## ANSWERS TO CHAPTER 15 EXERCISES (cont.)

**Ex. 13 (cont.)**

**2.**

 Name______________ Date______________

## ANSWERS TO CHAPTER 15 EXERCISES (cont.)

**Ex. 13 (cont.)**

**2. (cont.)**

 Name____________________ Date____________

## ANSWERS TO CHAPTER 15 EXERCISES (cont.)

**Ex. 13 (cont.)**

**3.**

### GENERAL JOURNAL

PAGE ________

| DATE 19—5 | | PARTICULARS | P.R. | DEBIT | CREDIT |
|---|---|---|---|---|---|
| | | | | | |
| | | | | | |
| | | | | | |
| | | | | | |
| | | | | | |
| | | | | | |
| | | | | | |
| | | | | | |
| | | | | | |

 Name________________ Date________

## ANSWERS TO CHAPTER 15 EXERCISES (cont.)

**Exercise 14, p. 669 (Workbook Exercise)**

Given below is the general ledger trial balance of Eastern Electronics as of June 30, 19–4, the end of a fiscal year.

EASTERN ELECTRONICS
TRIAL BALANCE
JUNE 30, 19–4

| | DR | CR |
|---|---|---|
| Bank | 1 555 20 | |
| Accounts Receivable | 26 200 50 | |
| Allowance for Doubtful Accounts | | 330 50 |
| Merchandise Inventory | 95 250 00 | |
| Supplies | 2 409 78 | |
| Prepaid Insurance | 2 654 00 | |
| Furniture and Equipment | 30 588 24 | |
| Accumulated Depreciation — Furn. & Equip. | | 14 927 06 |
| Automotive Equipment | 26 540 00 | |
| Accumulated Depreciation — Automotive Equipment | | 17 436 78 |
| Accounts Payable | | 8 541 02 |
| Sales Tax Payable | | 2 620 90 |
| Loan Payable — 12% | | 60 000 00 |
| S. Evans, Capital | | 26 595 47 |
| S. Evans, Drawings | 52 500 00 | |
| Sales | | 451 963 20 |
| Sales Returns and Allowances | 2 658 36 | |
| Discounts Earned | | 2 896 50 |
| Bank Charges | 752 15 | |
| Car Expense | 9 258 28 | |
| Discounts Allowed | 3 569 28 | |
| Duty | 2 560 25 | |
| Freight-in | 4 569 60 | |
| Interest on Loan | 5 400 00 | |
| Light, Heat, and Water | 3 850 24 | |
| Miscellaneous Expense | 1 264 65 | |
| Postage | 748 24 | |
| Purchases | 240 860 75 | |
| Purchases Returns and Allowances | | 14 692 54 |
| Rent | 15 000 00 | |
| Telephone | 2 858 00 | |
| Wages | 68 956 45 | |
| | 600 003 97 | 600 003 97 |

## ANSWERS TO CHAPTER 15 EXERCISES (cont.)

**Ex. 14 (cont.)**

1. **Using the additional information given below, complete the work sheet for the year ended June 30, 19-4.**

**Additional Information**

a. **Purchase invoices received subsequent to the year-end but pertaining to the fiscal period just ended are summarized as follows:**

| | |
|---|---|
| Supplies | $ 152.69 |
| Car Expenses | 375.52 |
| Miscellaneous Expense | 156.00 |
| Merchandise for Resale | 2 244.22 |
| Light and Heat | 268.00 |

b. **The accounts receivable aging schedule at June 30th showed doubtful debts totaling $1 502.40**

c. **Inventories at December 31, 19–5 are as follows:**

| | |
|---|---|
| Merchandise for Resale | $101 546.00 |
| Supplies | 1 420.60 |

d. **Details of insurance policies at December 31, 19–5 are as follows:**

| *Company* | *Policy Date* | *Term* | *Premium* |
|---|---|---|---|
| Southern | January 31, 19-4 | 1 year | $180.00 |
| Bonded | March 31, 19-4 | 1 year | 324.00 |
| Circle | September 30, 19-4 | 1 year | 840.00 |
| Global | June 1, 19-4 | 1 year | 84.00 |
| Central | December 1, 19-3 | 2 years | 144.00 |

e. **Depreciation is calculated on a declining-balance basis using government rates.**

f. **Wages for the two weeks ended Friday, July 3, amounted to $1 850.40. The employees work a five-day week and are paid for the July 1 holiday.**

g. **The anniversary date for the loan payable is March 31. Interest is due and payable annually on March 31.**

h. **An agreement states that the hired general manager is to receive a bonus if the net income (before taking the bonus into account) exceeds $50 000. The bonus is calculated at 10 per cent of the net income over $50 000 and is charged to Wages.**

2. **Prepare the balance sheet and the income statement.**

 Name______________ Date______________

## ANSWERS TO CHAPTER 15 EXERCISES (cont.)

**Ex. 14 (cont.)**

1.

Eastern Electronics

Work Sheet

| ACCOUNTS | TRIAL BALANCE DR | TRIAL BALANCE CR | ADJUSTMENTS DR | ADJUSTMENTS CR | INCOME STATEMENT DR | INCOME STATEMENT CR | BALANCE SHEET DR | BALANCE SHEET CR |
|---|---|---|---|---|---|---|---|---|
| Bank | 1 555 20 | | | | | | | |
| Accounts Receivable | 26 200 50 | | | | | | | |
| Allow. for Doubtful Debts | | 330 50 | | | | | | |
| Merchandise Inventory | 95 250 — | | | | | | | |
| Supplies | 2 409 78 | | | | | | | |
| Prepaid Insurance | 2 654 — | | | | | | | |
| Furniture and Equipment | 30 588 24 | | | | | | | |
| Accum. Deprec. Furn. & Equip. | | 14 927 06 | | | | | | |
| Automotive Equipment | 26 540 — | | | | | | | |
| Accum. Deprec. Auto. Equip. | | 17 436 78 | | | | | | |
| Accounts Payable | | 8 541 02 | | | | | | |
| Sales Tax Payable | | 2 620 90 | | | | | | |
| Loan Payable — 12% | | 60 000 — | | | | | | |
| S. Evans, Capital | | 26 595 47 | | | | | | |
| S. Evans, Drawings | 52 500 — | | | | | | | |
| Sales | | 451 963 20 | | | | | | |
| Sales Returns & Allowances | 2 658 36 | | | | | | | |
| Discounts Earned | | 2 896 50 | | | | | | |
| Bank Charges | 752 15 | | | | | | | |
| Car Expense | 9 258 28 | | | | | | | |
| Discounts Allowed | 3 569 28 | | | | | | | |
| Duty | 2 560 25 | | | | | | | |
| Freight-in | 4 569 60 | | | | | | | |
| Interest on Loan | 5 400 — | | | | | | | |
| Light, Heat, & Water | 3 850 24 | | | | | | | |
| Miscellaneous Expense | 1 264 65 | | | | | | | |
| Postage | 748 24 | | | | | | | |

## ANSWERS TO CHAPTER 15 EXERCISES (cont.)

**Ex. 14 (cont.)**

**1. (cont.)**

| Account | Debit | Credit |
|---|---|---|
| Purchases | 240 860 75 | |
| Purchases Returns & Allows. | | 14 692 54 |
| Rent | 15 000 — | |
| Telephone | 2 858 — | |
| Wages | 68 956 45 | |
| | 600 003 97 | 600 003 97 |

## ANSWERS TO CHAPTER 15 EXERCISES (cont.)

**Ex. 14 (cont.)**

**2.** ______________________________________________

______________________________________________

______________________________________________

 Name______________ Date______________

## ANSWERS TO CHAPTER 15 EXERCISES (cont.)

**Ex. 14 (cont.)**

**2. (cont.)**

## ANSWERS TO CHAPTER 15 EXERCISES (cont.)

### FOR FURTHER THOUGHT

**Exercise 15, p. 669**

1. ______________
2. ______________
3. ______________
4. ______________
5. ______________
6. ______________
7. ______________
8. ______________
9. ______________
10. ______________
11. ______________
12. ______________
13. ______________

## ANSWERS TO CHAPTER 15 EXERCISES (cont.)

**Ex. 15 (cont.)**

**14.** ______________________________

## CASE STUDIES (text, p. 670)

**Case 1** *Comparing Depreciation*, p. 670

| Year | Net Income Before Depreciation | Declining Balance at 30% | | | Straight-Line | | | Income Tax Gain (or loss) |
|---|---|---|---|---|---|---|---|---|
| | | Depreciation for Year | Net Income for Year | Income Tax at 40% | Depreciation for Year | Net Income for Year | Income Tax at 40% | |
| 1 | 75 000 – | | | | | | | |
| 2 | 75 000 – | | | | | | | |
| 3 | 80 000 – | | | | | | | |
| 4 | 82 000 – | | | | | | | |
| 5 | 85 000 – | | | | | | | |
| 6 | 85 000 – | | | | | | | |
| 7 | 90 000 – | | | | | | | |
| 8 | 90 000 – | | | | | | | |

**1.** ______________________________

**2.** ______________________________

**3.** ______________________________

**4.** ______________________________

**5.** ______________________________

# Chapter 15

Name________________________ Date____________

## CASE STUDIES (cont.)

**Case 2** *Banker Beware*, p. 671

1. ________________________

2. ________________________

3. ________________________

4. ________________________

5. ________________________

6. ________________________

**Case 3** *Meeting the Deadline*, p. 672

## CASE STUDIES (cont.)

### Case 3 (cont.)

*Stetsko and Company* — *Work Sheet* — *Six Months Ended June 30, 19—*

| ACCOUNTS | TRIAL BALANCE DR | TRIAL BALANCE CR | ADJUSTMENTS DR | ADJUSTMENTS CR | INCOME STATEMENT DR | INCOME STATEMENT CR | BALANCE SHEET DR | BALANCE SHEET CR |
|---|---|---|---|---|---|---|---|---|
| Bank | 4 172 50 | | | | | | | |
| Accounts Receivable | 27 421 – | | | | | | | |
| Supplies | 1 365 – | | | | | | | |
| Prepaid Insurance | 2 280 – | | | | | | | |
| Furniture and Equipment | 12 596 – | | | | | | | |
| Accum. Depr. Furn & Equip. | | 2 500 – | | | | | | |
| Automotive Equipment | 24 800 – | | | | | | | |
| Accum. Depr. Auto. Equip. | | 6 500 – | | | | | | |
| Accounts Payable | | 6 521 92 | | | | | | |
| Bank Loan | | 20 000 – | | | | | | |
| Sales Tax Payable | | 560 – | | | | | | |
| I. Stetsko, Capital | | 25 558 20 | | | | | | |
| I. Stetsko, Drawings | 15 000 – | | | | | | | |
| Sales | | 58 072 50 | | | | | | |
| Bank Charges | 1 132 10 | | | | | | | |
| Automotive Expense | 4 547 52 | | | | | | | |
| Miscellaneous Expense | 761 50 | | | | | | | |
| Rent | 2 600 – | | | | | | | |
| Telephone | 1 712 – | | | | | | | |
| Wages | 21 325 – | | | | | | | |
| | 119 712 62 | 119 712 62 | | | | | | |
| Depreciation Furn. & Equip. | | | | | | | | |
| Depreciation Auto. Equip. | | | | | | | | |
| Supplies Used | | | | | | | | |
| Insurance Expense | | | | | | | | |
| | | | | | | | | |
| Net Income | | | | | | | | |

## CASE STUDIES (cont.)

**Case 4** *Declining-Balance versus Distance-Used*, p. 673

The comparative depreciation schedule is shown below:

| Year | Distance Travelled | Depreciation Straight-line | Depreciation km travelled |
|---|---|---|---|
| 1 | 21 468 | | |
| 2 | 35 698 | | |
| 3 | 42 654 | | |
| 4 | 45 965 | | |
| 5 | 40 365 | | |
| 6 | 35 632 | | |
| 7 | 27 526 | | |
| 8 | 16 201 | | |
| Totals | 265 509 | | |

## ENTREPRENEUR Sonia Jones/Chairman, Peninsula Farm Ltd.

## ANSWERS TO DISCUSSION QUESTIONS (text, p. 674)

1. ____________________
2. ____________________
3. ____________________
4. ____________________

# Chapter 16 Partnership

## ANSWERS TO SECTION 16.1 REVIEW QUESTIONS (text, p. 680)

### Partnership: General Information

1. ______________________________

2. ______________________________

3. ______________________________

4. ______________________________

5. ______________________________

6. ______________________________

7. ______________________________

8. ______________________________

9. ______________________________

10. ______________________________

11. ______________________________

# Chapter 16

Name________________________ Date________________

## ANSWERS TO SECTION 16.1 EXERCISES (text, p. 680)

### Exercise 1, p. 680

Fill in the blanks with the most appropriate words or phrases to complete the following statements. A list of words and phrases is given below.

1. The partners of a business share in its ______ and _____.
2. There is a separate ______ account and ________ account for each partner.
3. You can usually tell if a business is a __________ from its name. You can also tell by examining its _____.
4. The day-by-day accounting for a partnership is no different than for a ____________.
5. Accounting for the partners' ______________ is the principal new aspect of partnership accounting.
6. The capital accounts of a partnership must be maintained in agreement with the terms of the ____________________.
7. Persons may pool their ________________ when forming a partnership.
8. Persons may bring together ________________ when forming a partnership.
9. Partnership provides a convenient way to keep a business in the _____.
10. Partners often give each other ________ support in regard to running a business.
11. A partnership is simple to _______.
12. A partnership is is not subject to ______________.
13. According to the law, a partnership is terminated by the death, incapacity, or _________ of any partner.
14. There is no ______________ in regard to partnership debts.
15. ______________ means that the partners are legally bound by the actions of any one of them.
16. The partnership agreement should be worked out with the help of a ______.
17. The ______________ of the various provinces come into play where there is no partnership agreement and a dispute arises.

| | |
|---|---|
| capital accounts | lawyer |
| capital | ledger |
| death | limited liability |
| different resources | losses |
| double taxation | mutual agency |
| drawings | organize |
| emotional support | partnership |
| family | Partnership Acts |
| financial resources | partnership agreement |
| incapacity | profits |
| insolvency | proprietorship |

# Chapter 16

Name ____________________ Date ____________

## ANSWERS TO SECTION 16.2 EXERCISES (text, p. 689)
## Accounting for Simple Partnership Formations

**Exercise 1, p. 689**

| 1. | | 1 | 2 | 3 | 4 | 5 | 6 | 7 | 8 |
|---|---|---|---|---|---|---|---|---|---|
| **a.** | Existing business? | | | | | | | | |
| **b.** | Capital amount? | | | | | | | | |
| **c.** | New business? | | | | | | | | |
| **d.** | New capital? | | | | | | | | |
| **e.** | Amount? | | | | | | | | |
| **f.** | Money changing hands privately? | | | | | | | | |
| **g.** | Amount? | | | | | | | | |
| **h.** | Total capital? | | | | | | | | |
| **i.** | Final capital ratios? | | | | | | | | |
| **j.** | Bonus? Who? | | | | | | | | |
| **k.** | Bonus? Amount? | | | | | | | | |

## ANSWERS TO SECTION 16.2 EXERCISES (cont.)

**Ex. 1 (cont.)**

**2.**

| DATE | PARTICULARS | P.R. | DEBIT | CREDIT |
|---|---|---|---|---|
| *1.* | | | | |
| | | | | |
| | | | | |
| | | | | |
| *2.* | | | | |
| | | | | |
| | | | | |
| | | | | |
| | | | | |
| *3.* | | | | |
| | | | | |
| | | | | |
| | | | | |
| | | | | |
| | | | | |
| | | | | |
| | | | | |
| *4.* | | | | |
| | | | | |
| | | | | |
| *5.* | | | | |
| | | | | |
| | | | | |
| *6.* | | | | |
| | | | | |
| | | | | |
| *7.* | | | | |
| | | | | |
| | | | | |
| | | | | |
| | | | | |
| *8.* | | | | |
| | | | | |
| | | | | |
| | | | | |
| | | | | |
| | | | | |
| | | | | |

 Name ____________ Date ____________

## ANSWERS TO SECTION 16.3 REVIEW QUESTIONS (text, p. 695)

## Apportionment of Net Income or Net Loss for a Partnership

1. ____________

2. ____________

3. ____________

5. ____________

6. ____________

7. ____________

8. ____________

9. ____________

10. ____________

11. ____________

12. ____________

13. ____________

14. ____________

15. ____________

## ANSWERS TO SECTION 16.3 EXERCISES (text, p. 696)

### Exercise 1, p. 696

Three partnership situations are described below. For each one, complete the chart to show how you would arrange for the partnership profits to be apportioned.

1. A and B operate a partnership in which:
   - — the two partners maintain equal capital account balances,
   - — both partners work full time in the business,
   - — neither partner has any special background or experience.

   Complete the chart.

| | |
|---|---|
| Give a salary to a partner or partners? Y or N? | |
| If yes, which one(s)? | |
| Give interest on capital balances? Y or N? | |
| Divide balance of net income equally? Y or N? | |
| If N, ratio to favour which partner(s)? | |

2. A and B form a partnership in which:
   - — A invests $200 000 in cash,<br>B invests $20 000 in cash.
   - — A does not participate at all in running the business,<br>B works full time in the business.
   - — A has many profitable business connections,<br>B has a great deal of experience and talent in the industry.

   Complete the chart.

| | |
|---|---|
| Give a salary to a partner or partners? Y or N? | |
| If yes, which one(s)? | |
| Give interest on capital balances? Y or N? | |
| Divide balance of net income equally? Y or N? | |
| If N, ratio to favour which partner(s)? | |

## ANSWERS TO SECTION 16.3 EXERCISES (cont.)

**Ex. 1 (cont.)**

**3.** A, B, and C form a partnership in which:

— A invests $500 000 cash in the business,
B invests $100 000 cash in the business,
C makes no financial investment.

— A and B do not work in the business in any way,
C works full time in the business.

— A and B have no experience, talent, or connections,
C is experienced, talented, and has connections.

Complete the chart.

| | |
|---|---|
| Give a salary to a partner or partners? Y or N? | |
| If yes, which one(s)? | |
| Give interest on capital balances? Y or N? | |
| Divide balance of net income equally? Y or N? | |
| If N, ratio to favour which partner(s)? | |

**Exercise 2, p. 697**

**a.** A B

**b.** A B

**c.** A B

## ANSWERS TO SECTION 16.3 EXERCISES (cont.)

**Ex. 2 (cont.)**

**d.** A B C

**e.** A B

**f.** A B C

**Exercise 3, p. 697**

**a.** A B

**b.** A B C

 Name ______________ Date ______________

## ANSWERS TO SECTION 16.4 REVIEW QUESTIONS (text, p. 706)
## Financial Statements for a Partnership

1. ______________
2. ______________
3. ______________
4. ______________
5. ______________
6. ______________
7. ______________
8. ______________
9. ______________
10. ______________
11. ______________
12. ______________

 Name________________ Date________

## ANSWERS TO SECTION 16.4 EXERCISES (text, p. 706)

**Exercise 1, p. 706**

1.

Li and Ahu

Statement of Distribution of Net Income

Year Ended December 31, 19–8

Li and Ahu

Statement of Partners' Capital

Year Ended December 31, 19–8

 Name________________ Date________

## ANSWERS TO SECTION 16.4 EXERCISES (cont.)

**Exercise 2, p. 707**

1.

General Associates

Statement of Distribution of Net Income

Year Ended December 31, 19–0

General Associates

Statement of Partners' Capital

Year Ended December 31, 19–0

## ANSWERS TO SECTION 16.4 EXERCISES (cont.)

**Ex. 2 (cont.)**

3.

General Associates
Balance Sheet
December 31, 19–0

4. **GENERAL JOURNAL** PAGE ______

# Chapter 16

Name________________ Date________________

## ANSWERS TO COMPUTER REVIEW 16.5 QUESTIONS (text, p. 711)

1. ____________________

2. ____________________

3. ____________________

4. ____________________

## COMMUNICATE IT (text, p. 711)

# Chapter 16

Name________________________ Date________________

## ANSWERS TO CHAPTER 16 EXERCISES (text, p. 712)

### USING YOUR KNOWLEDGE

**Exercise 1, p. 712**

**GENERAL JOURNAL** PAGE 1

| DATE 19— | | PARTICULARS | P.R. | DEBIT | CREDIT |
|---|---|---|---|---|---|
| | | | | | |

 Name_______________ Date_______

## ANSWERS TO CHAPTER 16 EXERCISES (cont.)

### Exercise 2, p. 713

GENERAL JOURNAL PAGE ______

| DATE | | PARTICULARS | P.R. | DEBIT | CREDIT |
|---|---|---|---|---|---|
| | | | | | |
| | | | | | |
| | | | | | |
| | | | | | |
| | | | | | |
| | | | | | |
| | | | | | |
| | | | | | |
| | | | | | |
| | | | | | |
| | | | | | |
| | | | | | |
| | | | | | |
| | | | | | |

### Exercise 3, p. 713

GENERAL JOURNAL PAGE ______

| DATE | | PARTICULARS | P.R. | DEBIT | CREDIT |
|---|---|---|---|---|---|
| | | | | | |
| | | | | | |
| | | | | | |
| | | | | | |
| | | | | | |
| | | | | | |
| | | | | | |
| | | | | | |
| | | | | | |
| | | | | | |
| | | | | | |
| | | | | | |
| | | | | | |
| | | | | | |
| | | | | | |

## ANSWERS TO CHAPTER 16 EXERCISES (cont.)

### Exercise 4, p. 713

GENERAL JOURNAL PAGE ______

| DATE | | PARTICULARS | P.R. | DEBIT | CREDIT |
|---|---|---|---|---|---|
| | | | | | |
| | | | | | |
| | | | | | |
| | | | | | |
| | | | | | |
| | | | | | |
| | | | | | |
| | | | | | |
| | | | | | |
| | | | | | |
| | | | | | |
| | | | | | |
| | | | | | |
| | | | | | |

### Exercise 5, p. 713

GENERAL JOURNAL PAGE ______

| DATE | | PARTICULARS | P.R. | DEBIT | CREDIT |
|---|---|---|---|---|---|
| | | | | | |
| | | | | | |
| | | | | | |
| | | | | | |
| | | | | | |
| | | | | | |
| | | | | | |
| | | | | | |
| | | | | | |
| | | | | | |
| | | | | | |
| | | | | | |
| | | | | | |
| | | | | | |

 Name________________ Date__________

## ANSWERS TO CHAPTER 16 EXERCISES (cont.)

**Exercise 6, p. 713**

GENERAL JOURNAL PAGE ______

| DATE | | PARTICULARS | P.R. | DEBIT | CREDIT |
|---|---|---|---|---|---|
| | | | | | |
| | | | | | |
| | | | | | |
| | | | | | |
| | | | | | |
| | | | | | |
| | | | | | |
| | | | | | |
| | | | | | |
| | | | | | |
| | | | | | |
| | | | | | |

**Exercise 7, p. 713**

| | Lemaire | Kennedy | Henning | Dudley |
|---|---|---|---|---|
| | | | | |
| | | | | |
| | | | | |
| | | | | |
| | | | | |
| | | | | |
| | | | | |
| | | | | |
| | | | | |
| | | | | |

**Exercise 8, p. 714**

| | Allen | Hamilton | Cooper | Cavanaugh |
|---|---|---|---|---|
| | | | | |
| | | | | |
| | | | | |
| | | | | |
| | | | | |
| | | | | |
| | | | | |

## ANSWERS TO CHAPTER 16 EXERCISES (cont.)

**Exercise 9, p. 714**

Barnes, Doby and Barnes

Statement of Distribution of Net Income

Year Ended April 30, 19–

**Exercise 10, p. 714**

Expert Investors

Statement of Distribution of Net Income

Year Ended June 30, 19–

 Name________________ Date____________

## ANSWERS TO CHAPTER 16 EXERCISES (cont.)

**Exercise 11, p. 714**

*Industrial Suppliers*

*Statement of Distribution of Net Income*

*Year Ended June 30, 19–*

| | | | | |
|---|---|---|---|---|
| | | | | |
| | | | | |
| | | | | |
| | | | | |
| | | | | |
| | | | | |
| | | | | |
| | | | | |
| | | | | |

## ANSWERS TO CHAPTER 16 EXERCISES (cont.)

**Exercise 12, p.715**

1.

Frame Brothers

Statement of Distribution of Net Income

Year Ended December 31, 19–

2.

Frame Brothers

Statement of Partners' Capital

Year Ended December 31, 19–

 Name________________ Date________

## ANSWERS TO CHAPTER 16 EXERCISES (cont.)

**Ex. 12 (cont.)**

3.

*Frame Brothers*

*Balance Sheet*

*December 31, 19—*

## ANSWERS TO CHAPTER 16 EXERCISES (cont.)

**Ex. 12 (cont.)**

4.

### GENERAL JOURNAL

PAGE ______

| DATE 19— | | PARTICULARS | P.R. | DEBIT | CREDIT |
|---|---|---|---|---|---|
| | | | | | |

## ANSWERS TO CHAPTER 16 EXERCISES (cont.)

**Exercise 13, p. 716**

1.

*Childs, Fogh and Hedman*

*Statement of Distribution of Net Income*

*Year Ended June 30, 19–5*

2.

*Childs, Fogh and Hedman*

*Statement of Partners' Capital*

*Year Ended June 30, 19–5*

## ANSWERS TO CHAPTER 16 EXERCISES (cont.)

**Ex. 13 (cont.)**

3.

*Childs, Fogh and Hedman*

*Balance Sheet*

*June 30, 19–5*

## ANSWERS TO CHAPTER 16 EXERCISES (cont.)

**Ex. 13 (cont.)**

4.

### GENERAL JOURNAL

PAGE ______

| DATE 19—5 | | PARTICULARS | P.R. | DEBIT | CREDIT |
|---|---|---|---|---|---|
| | | | | | |

## ANSWERS TO CHAPTER 16 EXERCISES (cont.)

**Exercise 14, p. 716**

1. ______
2. ______
3. ______
4. ______
5. ______
6. ______
7. ______
8. ______
9. ______
10. ______
11. ______

## CASE STUDIES (text, p.719)

**Case 1** *Keeping a Key Employee*, p. 719

1. ______
2. ______
3. ______
4. ______
5. ______
6. ______

# Chapter 16

Name____________________ Date__________

## CASE STUDIES (cont.)

**Case 2** *A Way out of a Cash Squeeze*, p. 720

**1.** 1. __________ **2.** 1. __________
2. __________ 2. __________
3. __________ 3. __________
4. __________ 4. __________
5. __________ 5. __________
6. __________ 6. __________
7. __________ 7. __________

**3.** __________

**Case 3** *A Problem of Sudden Termination*, p. 721

**1.** __________
**2.** __________
**3.** __________
**4.** __________
**5.** __________
**6.** __________
**7.** __________
**8.** __________
**9.** __________
**10.** __________
**11.** __________
**12.** __________

## CASE STUDIES (cont.)

**Case 4** *Partnership Agreement Unnecessary?*, p. 722

1. ______________________________
2. ______________________________
3. ______________________________
4. ______________________________

## ENTREPRENEUR Peggy Cole/Mmmarvellous Mmmuffins

### ANSWERS TO DISCUSSION QUESTIONS (text, p. 725)

1. ______________________________
2. ______________________________
3. ______________________________
4. ______________________________
5. ______________________________
6. ______________________________

# Chapter 17 Corporations

## ANSWERS TO SECTION 17.1 REVIEW QUESTIONS (text, p. 730)

### General Information

1. ____________________
2. ____________________
3. ____________________
4. ____________________
5. ____________________
6. ____________________
7. ____________________
8. ____________________
9. ____________________
10. ____________________
11. ____________________
12. ____________________
13. ____________________
14. ____________________
15. ____________________
16. ____________________
17. ____________________

# Chapter 17

Name_______________ Date_______________

## ANSWERS TO SECTION 17.1 EXERCISES (text, p. 730)

### Exercise 1, p. 730

1. ______________________________
2. ______________________________
3. ______________________________
4. ______________________________
5. ______________________________
6. ______________________________
7. ______________________________
8. ______________________________

### Exercise 2, p. 731

1. A corporation's capital is divided into ______ which are held by the shareholders.
2. The name of a corporation includes the word ______ or __________ or an accepted abbreviation of one of them.
3. Corporations were originally used for the purpose of raising large amounts of ______.
4. Each owner of a corporation receives a ______________ or ____________.
5. Only the _______ shares carry the privilege of ownership. Each one carries the right to ____.
6. An incorporated company is a __________________ in the eyes of the law.
7. In certain respects a corporation has the ______ and ________ of a real person.
8. The shareholders have no responsibility for _____ of the corporation beyond the amount required to pay for their shares. This is known as ______________.
9. If the scope of a company's operations is within a particular province, it will likely choose to operate under the _______________ for that province.
10. The _______________ is a committee of shareholders elected to manage the affairs of the company.
11. The day-by-day operations of a corporation are controlled by hired _________.
12. Permission to establish a corporation is given by the government in the form of a _______ or ___________.
13. A ________________ obtains its capital from the sale of bonds or shares to the general public.
14. A _________________ cannot have more than ____ shareholders.
15. The ________ of a corporation continues despite anything that happens to individual shareholders.
16. Shares of a public corporation may be easily acquired or disposed of through a ___________.

## ANSWERS TO SECTION 17.1 EXERCISES (cont.)

**Ex. 2 (cont.)**

17. The board of directors is elected at the ____________.
18. A corporation must pay its own __________. Thus the shareholders are subject to ____________ ________.

**Exercise 3, p. 732**

1. ____________________
2. ____________________
   ____________________
3. ____________________
4. ____________________
5. ____________________
6. ____________________
7. ____________________
   ____________________

## ANSWERS TO SECTION 17.2 REVIEW QUESTIONS (text, p. 735)

### Accounts of a Corporation

1. ____________________
   ____________________
2. ____________________
3. ____________________
4. ____________________
5. ____________________
6. ____________________
7. ____________________
8. ____________________
9. ____________________
10. ____________________
11. ____________________
12. ____________________
13. ____________________
14. ____________________

 Name________________ Date________

## ANSWERS TO SECTION 7.2 EXERCISES (text, p. 735)

**Exercise 1, p. 735**

A corporation began business on January 1, 19–1. Over the next seven years it made profits and paid out dividends as shown in the chart below.

Complete the Retained Earnings column of the chart.

| Year | Profits (Losses) | Dividends Paid | Retained Earnings at Year-end |
|---|---|---|---|
| 1 | ($45 000) | nil | |
| 2 | ($20 000) | nil | |
| 3 | $ 25 000 | nil | |
| 4 | $ 48 000 | nil | |
| 5 | $110 000 | $50 000 | |
| 6 | $156 000 | $100 000 | |
| 7 | $227 000 | $120 000 | |

Answer the following questions.

1. Why were no dividends paid in the first three years?

   Answer: ________________

2. Could a dividend have been paid in year 4?

   Answer: ________________

3. In your opinion, why was dividend not paid in year 4?

   Answer: ________________

4. All of the retained earnings were not paid out in dividends. Give reasons why this would be the case.

   Answer: ________________

## ANSWERS TO SECTION 17. 2 EXERCISES (cont.)

**Exercise 2, p. 736**

| Mandrell Limited<br>Balance Sheet<br>December 31, 19-6 |
|---|
| |
| |
| |
| |
| |
| |
| |
| |
| |
| |
| |
| |
| |
| |
| |
| |
| |
| |
| |
| |

**Exercise 3, p. 736**

1. ____________________
2. ____________________
3. ____________________
4. ____________________

# Chapter 17

Name ______________________ Date ______________

## ANSWERS TO SECTION 17.3 REVIEW QUESTIONS (text, p. 738)

### Dividends

1. ______________________________

2. ______________________________
3. ______________________________
4. ______________________________

5. ______________________________

6. ______________________________

7. ______________________________

8. ______________________________
9. ______________________________
10. ______________________________

11. ______________________________

12. ______________________________

## ANSWERS TO SECTION 17.3 EXERCISES (text, p. 738)

**Exercise 1, p. 738**

1. ______________________________
2. ______________________________
3. ______________________________
4. ______________________________

 Name____________________ Date____________

## ANSWERS TO SECTION 17.3 EXERCISES (cont.)

### Exercise 2, p. 739

1. A dividend is distributed to the __________ in proportion to the number of shares held.
2. Retained Earnings represents the company's net __________ of earnings.
3. Only the __________ has the power to declare a dividend.
4. When dividends are declared they are declared to __________ on a certain date.
5. A good system is necessary for keeping __________ up to date and accurate.
6. __________ are usually stated at so much a share.
7. Once declared, a dividend becomes a __________ of the company.
8. The Retained Earnings account normally has a _____ balance.
9. When a dividend is declared it is set up in a __________ account.
10. When a dividend is declared, the __________ account is reduced.

### Exercise 3, p. 739

Complete the schedule shown below for a company whose fiscal year ends on December 31.

| *Year* | *Number Shares Sold* | *Cumulative Number Shares Issued* | *Income for Year* | *Dividend Declared Dec. 15* | *Total Dividend For Year* | *Retained Earnings Dec 31* |
|---|---|---|---|---|---|---|
| 1 | 10 000 | | $52 500 | $1.00 | | |
| 2 | 12 000 | | $50 250 | $1.50 | | |
| 3 | 12 500 | | $60 750 | $1.60 | | |
| 4 | 15 000 | | $75 200 | $1.75 | | |
| 5 | 20 000 | | $95 050 | $1.85 | | |

### Exercise 4, p. 739

1. ____________________
2. ____________________
3. ____________________

# Chapter 17

Name________________________ Date____________

## ANSWERS TO SECTION 17.4 REVIEW QUESTIONS (text, p. 744)

## Accounting for the Issue of Shares and for Organization Costs

1. ______________________________
2. ______________________________
3. ______________________________
4. ______________________________
5. ______________________________
6. ______________________________
7. ______________________________
8. ______________________________
9. ______________________________

## ANSWERS TO SECTION 17.4 EXERCISES (text, p. 744)

### Exercise 1, p. 744

1. ______________________________
2. ______________________________
3. ______________________________
4. ______________________________
5. ______________________________

### Exercise 2, p. 745

1. The proceeds from the sale of shares are credited to a Capital Stock account. ☐
2. A corporation is allowed to have only one Capital Stock account. ☐
3. The legal fees paid to a lawyer for services in setting up the corporation are an organization cost. ☐
4. Organization costs are debited directly to an expense account. ☐
5. Every share certificate of a corporation carries the right to one vote. ☐
6. Each class of capital stock must be kept in a separate account. ☐
7. At the annual meeting preferred shareholders vote before the common shareholders. ☐
8. Preferred stock is issued so that common shareholders can retain their control of the corporation. ☐

## ANSWERS TO SECTION 17.4 EXERCISES (cont.)

**Ex. 2 (cont.)**

9. Usually, a preferred dividend is limited to a specific amount. ☐
10. Preferred dividends are paid annually without fail. ☐
11. The par value of a share is the amount it must be sold for. ☐
12. It is now common practice to issue shares that have no par value. ☐

**Explanations**

2. ______________________________
4. ______________________________
5. ______________________________
______________________________
7. ______________________________
10. ______________________________
______________________________
11. ______________________________
______________________________
______________________________

## ANSWERS TO SECTION 17.4 EXERCISES (cont.)

**Exercise 3, p. 745 Opra Corporation**

1. **GENERAL JOURNAL** PAGE ________

| DATE 19—6 | | PARTICULARS | P.R. | DEBIT | CREDIT |
|---|---|---|---|---|---|
| | | | | | |

## ANSWERS TO SECTION 17.4 EXERCISES (cont.)

**Ex. 3 (cont.)**

**2.**

Bank

Land

Common Stock

Organization Costs

Building

**a.** ______________________________

**b.** ______________________________

**c.** ______________________________

**3.**

Opra Corporation
Balance Sheet
February 22, 19–6

## ANSWERS TO SECTION 17.4 EXERCISES (cont.)

**Exercise 4, p. 746 Wonder World Limited**

1\. GENERAL JOURNAL PAGE ______

| DATE 19— | | PARTICULARS | P.R. | DEBIT | CREDIT |
|---|---|---|---|---|---|
| | | | | | |

## ANSWERS TO SECTION 17.4 EXERCISES (cont.)

**Ex. 4 (cont.)**

**2.**

Bank

Land

Common Stock

Plant and Equipment

Organization Costs

Preferred Stock 8%

Wonder World Limited
Balance Sheet
June 30, 19—

## ANSWERS TO SECTION 17.4 EXERCISES (cont.)

**Exercise 5, p. 746 Regus Corporation**

1.

Bank

Dividends Payable

Common Stock

Land

Preferred Stock $5

Building

Retained Earnings

Other Assets

Organization Costs

 Name____________________ Date__________

## ANSWERS TO SECTION 17.4 EXERCISES (cont.)

**Ex. 5 (cont.)**

**2.**

Regus Corporation
Balance Sheet
–date–

| | | |
|---|---|---|
| | | |
| | | |
| | | |
| | | |
| | | |
| | | |
| | | |
| | | |
| | | |
| | | |
| | | |
| | | |
| | | |
| | | |
| | | |
| | | |

## ANSWERS TO SECTION 17.5 REVIEW QUESTIONS (text, p. 749)

## Types of Preferred Shares

**1.** ____________________

**2.** ____________________

**3.** ____________________

**4.** ____________________

**5.** ____________________

# Chapter 17

Name________________________ Date________________

## ANSWERS TO SECTION 17.5 EXERCISES (text, p. 749)

### Exercise 1, p. 749

| ABC Limited *Year* | *Total Dividend* | *Common Dividend* | *Preferred Dividend* |
|---|---|---|---|
| 1 | nil | | |
| 2 | $100 000 | | |
| 3 | $100 000 | | |
| 4 | nil | | |
| 5 | $ 50 000 | | |
| 6 | $120 000 | | |
| 7 | $150 000 | | |

### Exercise 2, p. 750

| PQ Limited *Year* | *Total Dividend* | *Common Dividend* | *Preferred Dividend* |
|---|---|---|---|
| 1 | $50 000 | | |
| 2 | $70 000 | | |
| 3 | nil | | |
| 4 | $50 000 | | |
| 5 | $70 000 | | |

### Exercise 3, p. 750

| ABCD Limited *Year* | *Total Dividend* | *Common Dividend* | *Preferred Dividend* |
|---|---|---|---|
| 1 | $150 000 | | |
| 2 | $150 000 | | |
| 3 | $210 000 | | |
| 4 | $240 000 | | |
| 5 | $270 000 | | |

## ANSWERS TO SECTION 17.5 EXERCISES (cont.)

**Exercise 4, p. 750**

1.

| XYZ Limited *Year* | *Total Dividend* | *Common Dividend* | *Preferred Dividend* |
|---|---|---|---|
| 1 | $ 90 000 | | |
| 2 | $ 80 000 | | |
| 3 | nil | | |
| 4 | $190 000 | | |
| 5 | $120 000 | | |
| 6 | $140 000 | | |
| 7 | $148 000 | | |
| 8 | nil | | |
| 9 | $250 000 | | |
| 10 | $240 000 | | |

2.

| XYZ Limited *Year* | *Total Dividend* | *Common Dividend* | *Preferred Dividend* |
|---|---|---|---|
| 1 | $ 90 000 | | |
| 2 | $ 80 000 | | |
| 3 | nil | | |
| 4 | $190 000 | | |
| 5 | $120 000 | | |
| 6 | $140 000 | | |
| 7 | $148 000 | | |
| 8 | nil | | |
| 9 | $250 000 | | |
| 10 | $240 000 | | |

 Name ____________ Date ____________

## ANSWERS TO SECTION 17.6 REVIEW QUESTIONS (text, p. 755)

### Equity Section of the Balance Sheet for a Corporation

1. ____________

2. ____________

3. ____________

4. ____________

5. ____________

6. ____________

7. ____________

8. ____________

9. ____________

10. ____________

11. ____________

12. ____________

# Chapter 17

Name________________________ Date____________

## ANSWERS TO SECTION 17.6 EXERCISES (text, p. 755)

**Exercise 1, p. 755**

AKO Corporation

*Shareholders' Equity*

**Exercise 2, p. 756**

Mainmast Limited

*Shareholders' Equity*

**Exercise 3, p. 756**

Lebrun Corporation

**1.**

**2.** *Shareholders' Equity*

## ANSWERS TO SECTION 17.6 EXERCISES (cont.)

**Exercise 4, p. 756**

## ANSWERS TO SECTION 17.7 REVIEW QUESTIONS (text, p. 762)

**Income Tax for Corporations**

1. 
2. 
3. 
4. 
5. 
6. 
7. 
8. 
9. 
10. 

## ANSWERS TO SECTION 17.7 EXERCISES (text, p. 762)

### Exercise 1, p. 762

A simple work sheet is completed below except for the income tax. Given that the corporate rate of income tax is 38 per cent, finish off the work sheet.

Little Company Limited | Work Sheet | Year Ended Dec. 31, 19–7

| Accounts | Trial Balance | | Adjustments | | Income Statement | | Balance Sheet | |
|---|---|---|---|---|---|---|---|---|
| | Dr | Cr | Dr | Cr | Dr | Cr | Dr | Cr |
| Asset A | 50 | | | | | | 50 | |
| Asset B | 100 | | | | | | 100 | |
| Asset C | 1 000 | | | | | | 1 000 | |
| Asset D | 10 000 | | | | | | 10 000 | |
| Liability A | | 500 | | | | | | 500 |
| Liability B | | 1 000 | | | | | | 1 000 |
| Capital Stock | | 5 000 | | | | | | 5 000 |
| Retained Earnings | | 2 150 | | | | | | 2 150 |
| Revenue | | 10 000 | | | | 10 000 | | |
| Expense A | 1 000 | | | | 1 000 | | | |
| Expense B | 3 000 | | | | 3 000 | | | |
| Expense C | 2 000 | | | | 2 000 | | | |
| Income Tax Expense | 1 500 | | | | | | | |
| | 18 650 | 18 650 | | | | | | |
| Income Tax Payable | | | | | | | | |
| | | | | | | | | |
| Net Income | | | | | | | | |
| | | | | | | | | |
| | | | | | | | | |

Name______________ Date______________

## ANSWERS TO SECTION 17.7 EXERCISES (cont.)

**Exercise 2, p. 763**

1.

Giant Company limited — Work Sheet — Year Ended Dec. 31, 19–8

| ACCOUNTS | TRIAL BALANCE DR | TRIAL BALANCE CR | ADJUSTMENTS DR | ADJUSTMENTS CR | INCOME STATEMENT DR | INCOME STATEMENT CR | BALANCE SHEET DR | BALANCE SHEET CR |
|---|---|---|---|---|---|---|---|---|
| Bank | 4 003 — | | | | | | | |
| Accs. Receivable | 40 201 — | | | | | | | |
| Supplies | 941 — | | | | | | | |
| Equipment | 63 666 — | | | | | | | |
| Acc. Depr. Equip. | | 18 356 — | | | | | | |
| Accs. Payable | | 1 241 — | | | | | | |
| Capital Stock | | 20 000 — | | | | | | |
| Retained Earnings | | 33 091 — | | | | | | |
| Revenue | | 119 044 — | | | | | | |
| Advertising | 3 742 — | | | | | | | |
| Bank Charges | 1 502 — | | | | | | | |
| Income Tax Exp. | 18 000 — | | | | | | | |
| Light and Heat | 4 016 — | | | | | | | |
| Misc. Expense | 1 240 — | | | | | | | |
| Rent | 16 000 — | | | | | | | |
| Telephone | 2 519 — | | | | | | | |
| Wages | 35 902 — | | | | | | | |
| | 191 735 — | 191 732 — | | | | | | |
| Deprec. Equip. | | | | | | | | |
| Supplies Used | | | | | | | | |
| Inc. Tax Rec'l | | | | | | | | |
| | | | | | | | | |
| Net Income | | | | | | | | |

 Name______________________ Date______________

## ANSWERS TO SECTION 17.7 EXERCISES (cont.)

**Ex. 2. (cont.)**

2. **GENERAL JOURNAL** PAGE ________

| DATE 19—8 | PARTICULARS | P.R. | DEBIT | CREDIT |
|---|---|---|---|---|
| | | | | |

 Name________________ Date__________

## ANSWERS TO CHAPTER 17 EXERCISES (text, p. 765)

### USING YOUR KNOWLEDGE

**Exercise 1, p. 765 Parks Company Limited**

1.

GENERAL JOURNAL PAGE ______

| DATE 19—1 | PARTICULARS | P.R. | DEBIT | CREDIT |
|---|---|---|---|---|
| 1. | | | | |
| | | | | |
| | | | | |
| | | | | |
| | | | | |
| 2. | | | | |
| | | | | |
| | | | | |
| | | | | |
| 3. | | | | |
| | | | | |
| | | | | |
| | | | | |
| 4. | | | | |
| | | | | |
| | | | | |
| | | | | |
| 5. | | | | |
| | | | | |
| | | | | |
| | | | | |
| 6. | | | | |
| | | | | |
| | | | | |
| | | | | |
| | | | | |
| | | | | |
| 7. | | | | |
| | | | | |
| | | | | |
| | | | | |
| 8. | | | | |
| | | | | |
| | | | | |
| | | | | |
| | | | | |

 Name________________ Date________________

## ANSWERS TO CHAPTER 17 EXERCISES (cont.)

**Ex. 1 (cont.)**

**1. (cont.)**

### GENERAL JOURNAL

PAGE ______

| DATE 19—2 | | PARTICULARS | P.R. | DEBIT | CREDIT |
|---|---|---|---|---|---|
| 9. | | | | | |
| | | | | | |
| | | | | | |
| | | | | | |
| 10. | | | | | |
| | | | | | |
| | | | | | |
| | | | | | |
| | | | | | |
| 11. | | | | | |
| | | | | | |
| | | | | | |
| 12. | | | | | |
| | | | | | |
| | | | | | |
| 19—3 | | | | | |
| 13. | | | | | |
| | | | | | |
| | | | | | |
| | | | | | |
| 14. | | | | | |
| | | | | | |
| | | | | | |
| | | | | | |
| | | | | | |
| | | | | | |

2.

| | | Trial Balance | | | |
|---|---|---|---|---|---|
| | | | | | |
| | | | | | |
| | | | | | |
| | | | | | |
| | | | | | |
| | | | | | |
| | | | | | |
| | | | | | |
| | | | | | |
| | | | | | |
| | | | | | |

## ANSWERS TO CHAPTER 17 EXERCISES (cont.)

**Exercise 2, p. 765 Sentra Loan Corporation**

1.

### GENERAL JOURNAL

PAGE ______

| DATE 19—1 | PARTICULARS | P.R. | DEBIT | CREDIT |
| --- | --- | --- | --- | --- |
| 1. | | | | |
| 2. | | | | |
| 3. | | | | |
| 4. | | | | |
| 5. | | | | |
| 6. | | | | |
| 7. | | | | |

## ANSWERS TO CHAPTER 17 EXERCISES (cont.)

**Ex. 2 (cont.) Sentra Loan Corporation**

**1. (cont.)**

### GENERAL JOURNAL

PAGE ________

| DATE 19—2 | | PARTICULARS | P.R. | DEBIT | CREDIT |
|---|---|---|---|---|---|
| 8. | | | | | |
| 9. | | | | | |
| 10. | | | | | |
| 11. | | | | | |
| 12. | | | | | |
| 19—3 | | | | | |
| 13. | | | | | |
| 14. | | | | | |
| 15. | | | | | |

 Name ____________ Date ____________

## ANSWERS TO CHAPTER 17 EXERCISES (cont.)

**Ex. 2 (cont.) Sentra Loan Corporation**

1. (cont.)

### GENERAL JOURNAL

PAGE ______

| DATE 19—3 | | PARTICULARS | P.R. | DEBIT | CREDIT |
|---|---|---|---|---|---|
| | 16. | | | | |
| | | | | | |
| | | | | | |
| 19—4 | | | | | |
| | 17. | | | | |
| | | | | | |
| | | | | | |
| | | | | | |
| | 18. | | | | |
| | | | | | |
| | | | | | |
| | | | | | |
| | 19. | | | | |
| | | | | | |
| | | | | | |
| | | | | | |
| 2. | | TRIAL BALANCE | | | |

## ANSWERS TO CHAPTER 17 EXERCISES (cont.)

**Exercise 3, p. 766 Maxwell Limited**

**1.** ____________________

**2.** ____________________

**3.**

GENERAL JOURNAL PAGE ____

| DATE 19— | | PARTICULARS | P.R. | DEBIT | CREDIT |
|---|---|---|---|---|---|
| | | | | | |
| | | | | | |
| | | | | | |
| | | | | | |
| | | | | | |
| | | | | | |
| | | | | | |
| | | | | | |
| | | | | | |

**4.**

 Name________________ Date________________

## ANSWERS TO CHAPTER 17 EXERCISES (cont.)

**Exercise 4, p. 766 EFG Co. Ltd.**

### GENERAL JOURNAL

PAGE ________

| DATE 19— | PARTICULARS | P.R. | DEBIT | CREDIT |
|---|---|---|---|---|
| | | | | |

 Name______________________ Date____________

## ANSWERS TO CHAPTER 17 EXERCISES (cont.)

**Exercise 5, p. 767 Vintage Products Limited**

### GENERAL JOURNAL

PAGE ______

| DATE 19— | | PARTICULARS | P.R. | DEBIT | CREDIT |
|---|---|---|---|---|---|
| 1. | | | | | |
| 2. | | | | | |
| 3. | | | | | |
| 4. | | | | | |

 Name________________ Date____________

## ANSWERS TO CHAPTER 17 EXERCISES (cont.)

### Exercise 6, p. 767

| Year | Amount | Non-Cumulative Stock | | Cumulative Stock | |
|---|---|---|---|---|---|
| | | Common | Preferred | Common | Preferred |
| 1 | $70 000 | | | | |
| 2 | nil | | | | |
| 3 | 40 000 | | | | |
| 4 | 5 000 | | | | |
| 5 | 55 000 | | | | |
| 6 | 80 000 | | | | |
| 7 | 15 000 | | | | |
| 8 | 45 000 | | | | |

### Exercise 7, p. 768 E-Z Limited

| Year | Amount | Non-Participating | | Fully Participating | |
|---|---|---|---|---|---|
| | | Common | Preferred | Common | Preferred |
| 1 | $ 60 000 | | | | |
| 2 | $ 75 000 | | | | |
| 3 | nil | | | | |
| 4 | $120 000 | | | | |
| 5 | $180 000 | | | | |
| 6 | nil | | | | |
| 7 | $135 000 | | | | |
| 8 | $ 90 000 | | | | |
| 9 | $100 000 | | | | |
| 10 | $150 000 | | | | |

## ANSWERS TO CHAPTER 17 EXERCISES (cont.)

### Exercise 8, p. 768 Alpine Products

### Exercise 9, p. 768 Kingston Investments

Name________________ Date________________

## ANSWERS TO CHAPTER 17 EXERCISES (cont.)

**Exercise 10, p. 768 Sesco Limited**

1.

*Sesco Limited* — *Work Sheet* — *Yr Ended Dec. 31, 19—*

| ACCOUNTS | TRIAL BALANCE DR | TRIAL BALANCE CR | ADJUSTMENTS DR | ADJUSTMENTS CR | INCOME STATEMENT DR | INCOME STATEMENT CR | BALANCE SHEET DR | BALANCE SHEET CR |
|---|---|---|---|---|---|---|---|---|
| Petty Cash | 100 — | | | | | | 100 — | |
| Bank | 1 462 — | | | | | | 1 462 — | |
| Accounts Receivable | 29 053 74 | | | | | | 29 053 74 | |
| Allow. Doubtful Accs. | | 750 80 | | 652 20 | | | | 1 403 — |
| Merchandise Inventory | 21 416 — | | | | 21 416 — | 28 331 50 | 28 331 50 | |
| Supplies | 1 470 — | | | 864 — | | | 606 — | |
| Prepaid Insurance | 2 798 — | | | 1 562 — | | | 1 236 — | |
| Land | 42 200 46 | | | | | | 42 200 46 | |
| Buildings | 95 900 — | | | | | | 95 900 — | |
| Accum. Depr. Buildings | | 13 677 74 | | 4 111 11 | | | | 17 788 85 |
| Furniture & Equipment | 42 750 — | | | | | | 42 750 — | |
| Acc. Depr. Furn. & Equip. | | 20 862 — | | 4 377 60 | | | | 25 239 60 |
| Automotive Equipment | 29 750 — | | | | | | 29 750 — | |
| Accum. Depr. Auto. Equip. | | 19 545 75 | | 3 061 28 | | | | 22 607 03 |
| Accounts Payable | | 46 315 15 | | 3 072 40 | | | | 49 387 55 |
| Bank Loan | | 11 000 — | | | | | | 11 000 — |
| Sales Tax Payable | | 1 032 01 | | | | | | 1 032 01 |
| Capital Stock | | 100 000 — | | | | | | 100 000 — |
| Retained Earnings | | 26 225 42 | | | | | | 26 225 42 |
| Sales | | 196 917 62 | | | | 196 917 62 | | |
| Bank Charges | 915 — | | | | 915 — | | | |
| Building Maintenance | 1 206 — | | | | 1 206 — | | | |
| Car Expenses | 1 815 70 | | | | 1 815 70 | | | |
| Duty | 3 741 11 | | 1 057 — | | 4 798 11 | | | |
| Freight-in | 1 707 — | | 916 — | | 2 623 — | | | |
| Income Tax Expense | 24 000 — | | | | | | | |

## ANSWERS TO CHAPTER 17 EXERCISES (cont.)

**Ex. 10 (cont.) Sesco Limited**

| Account | | | | |
|---|---|---|---|---|
| Light, Heat, Water | 1 946.70 | | | 1 946.70 |
| Miscellaneous Expense | 315.77 | | 75.— | 390.77 |
| Purchases | 75 647.— | | 1 024.40 | 76 671.40 |
| Telephone Expense | 1 217.81 | | | 1 217.81 |
| Wages | 56 914.20 | | | 56 914.20 |
| | 436 326.49 | 436 326.49 | | |
| Bad Debts Expense | | | 652.20 | 652.20 |
| Supplies Used | | | 864.— | 864.— |
| Insurance Expense | | | 1 562.— | 1 562.— |
| Depreciation Buildings | | | 4 111.11 | 4 111.11 |
| Depr. Furn. & Equip. | | | 4 377.60 | 4 377.60 |
| Depr. Auto. Equip. | | | 3 061.28 | 3 061.28 |
| Income Tax Receivable | | | | |
| Net Income | | | | |

## ANSWERS TO CHAPTER 17 EXERCISES (cont.)

**Ex. 10 (cont.)**

**2.**

Sesco Limited

Income Statement

Year Ended December 31, 19—

 Name________________________ Date____________

## ANSWERS TO CHAPTER 17 EXERCISES (cont.)

**Ex. 10 (cont.)**

Sesco Limited

**2. (cont.)**

Balance Sheet

December 31, 19–

 Name ____________ Date ____________

## ANSWERS TO CHAPTER 17 EXERCISES (cont.)

**Ex. 10 (cont.)**

3.

### GENERAL JOURNAL

PAGE ________

| DATE 19— | | PARTICULARS | P.R. | DEBIT | CREDIT |
|---|---|---|---|---|---|
| | | | | | |

 Name __________ Date __________

## ANSWERS TO CHAPTER 17 EXERCISES (cont.)

**Ex. 10 (cont.)**

**3. (cont.)**

GENERAL JOURNAL PAGE ______

| DATE 19— | | PARTICULARS | P.R. | DEBIT | CREDIT |
|---|---|---|---|---|---|
| | | | | | |

Name____________________ Date______________

## ANSWERS TO CHAPTER 17 EXERCISES (cont.)

### Exercise 11, p. 769 Alice Harper and Associates Limited

The partially completed work sheet for Alice Harper and Associates Limited appears below. The trial balance columns have been entered for you.

Using the additional information provided below, complete the work sheet for the year ended December 31, 19–5.

**Additional Information**

1. The allowance for doubtful accounts should be $850 at the year-end.
2. The year-end supplies inventory is $850.
3. The prepaid insurance figure at the year-end is $500.
4. The depreciation figures for the year are:

   | | |
   |---|---|
   | Buildings | — $3 000 |
   | Furniture and Equipment | — $2 500 |
   | Automotive Equipment | — $7 000 |

5. Accrued wages at the year-end amounted to $900.
6. $700 is to be written off the Organization Costs account.
7. The income tax rate is 40 per cent.

Work Sheet Alice Harper and Associates Limited Year Ended December 31, 19–5

| ACCOUNTS | TRIAL BALANCE | | ADJUSTMENTS | | INCOME STATEMENT | | BALANCE SHEET | |
|---|---|---|---|---|---|---|---|---|
| | DR | CR | DR | CR | DR | CR | DR | CR |
| Bank | 9 000 00 | | | | | | | |
| Accounts Receivable | 24 400 00 | | | | | | | |
| Allowance Doubtful Debts | | 200 00 | | | | | | |
| Supplies | 1 475 00 | | | | | | | |
| Prepaid Insurance | 1 260 00 | | | | | | | |
| Land | 95 690 00 | | | | | | | |
| Buildings | 120 000 00 | | | | | | | |
| Accum. Deprec. Buildings | | 24 000 00 | | | | | | |
| Furniture and Equipment | 38 000 00 | | | | | | | |
| Accum. Depr. Furn. & Equip. | | 20 000 00 | | | | | | |
| Automotive Equipment | 38 000 00 | | | | | | | |
| Accum. Deprec. Auto. Equip. | | 14 000 00 | | | | | | |
| Organization Costs | 4 200 00 | | | | | | | |
| Accounts Payable | | 15 700 00 | | | | | | |
| Sales Tax Payable | | 938 00 | | | | | | |
| Capital Stock, Common | | 25 000 00 | | | | | | |
| Capital Stock, 8% Preferred | | 100 000 00 | | | | | | |
| Retained Earnings | | 7 287 00 | | | | | | |

Name________________________ Date____________________

## ANSWERS TO CHAPTER 17 EXERCISES (cont.)

### Ex. 11 (cont.)

| Account | Debit | Credit |
|---|---|---|
| Fees Earned | | 160 800 00 |
| Advertising | 1 850 00 | |
| Bank Charges | 2 750 00 | |
| C.P.P. Expense | 750 00 | |
| Income Tax Expense | 5 600 00 | |
| Light, Heat, Water | 1 650 00 | |
| Miscellaneous Expense | 175 00 | |
| Postage | 500 00 | |
| Telephone | 1 025 00 | |
| U. I. Expense | 300 00 | |
| Wages | 29 400 00 | |
| | 367 925 00 | 367 925 00 |
| Bad Debts Expense | | |
| Supplies Used | | |
| Insurance Expense | | |
| Depreciation Building | | |
| Depreciation Furn. & Equip. | | |
| Depreciation Auto. Equip. | | |
| Accrued Wages Payable | | |
| Organiz'n Costs Written Off | | |
| Income Tax Payable | | |
| | | |
| Net Income | | |

## ANSWERS TO CHAPTER 17 EXERCISES (cont.)

**Exercise 12, p. 772 Rollins Limited**

1. ____________________
2. ____________________
3. ____________________
4. ____________________

**Exercise 13, p. 772 ABC Company**

1. ____________________
2. ____________________
3. ____________________
4. ____________________
5. ____________________
6. ____________________
7. ____________________
8. ____________________
9. ____________________
10. ____________________
11. ____________________
12. ____________________

 Name______________________ Date______________

## ANSWERS TO CHAPTER 17 EXERCISES (cont.)

**Exercise 14, p. 773 Master Products Limited**

### GENERAL JOURNAL

PAGE ________

| DATE 19— | | PARTICULARS | P.R. | DEBIT | CREDIT |
|---|---|---|---|---|---|
| **1.** | | | | | |
| | | | | | |
| | | | | | |
| | | | | | |
| **2.** | | | | | |
| | | | | | |
| | | | | | |
| | | | | | |
| | | | | | |
| | | | | | |
| **3. a.** | | | | | |
| | | | | | |
| | | | | | |
| | | | | | |
| | | | | | |
| **b.** | | | | | |
| | | | | | |
| | | | | | |
| | | | | | |
| | | | | | |
| | | | | | |
| | | | | | |
| | | | | | |
| | | | | | |
| | | | | | |
| | | | | | |
| | | | | | |
| | | | | | |
| | | | | | |
| | | | | | |
| | | | | | |
| | | | | | |

## ANSWERS TO CHAPTER 17 EXERCISES (cont.)

**Ex. 14 (cont.)**

**4. a.** ______________________________

**b.** ______________________________

**5.** ______________________________

### FOR FURTHER THOUGHT

**Exercise 15, p. 774**

**1.** ______________________________

**2.** ______________________________

**3.** ______________________________

 Name____________________ Date____________

## ANSWERS TO CHAPTER 17 EXERCISES (cont.)

**Ex. 15 (cont.)**

4.

5.

6.

7.

8.

9.

10.

11.

12.

## CASE STUDIES (text, p. 775)

**Case 1** *Should Dividends Be Declared?*, p. 775

1.
2.
3.
4.
5.
6.
7.

## CASE STUDIES (cont.)

8. ____________________

9. ____________________

**Case 2** *Buy the Shares or the Assets?*, p. 776

1. ____________________
2. ____________________
3. ____________________
4. ____________________

**Case 3** *Control of a Corporation*, p. 776

1. ____________________
2. ____________________
3. ____________________
4. ____________________
5. ____________________
6. ____________________
7. ____________________

 Name ______________ Date ______________

## CAREER Kim Brady/Financial Analyst

### ANSWERS TO DISCUSSION QUESTIONS (text, p. 779)

1. ______________

2. ______________

3. ______________

4. ______________

5. ______________

6. ______________

# Chapter 18 Analyzing Financial Statements

## ANSWERS TO SECTION 18.1 REVIEW QUESTIONS (text, p. 781)
### Users of Financial Statements

1. ____________________
2. ____________________
3. ____________________
4. ____________________
5. ____________________
6. ____________________
7. ____________________
8. ____________________
9. ____________________

## ANSWERS TO SECTION 18.2 REVIEW QUESTIONS (text, p. 791)
### Comparing Financial Data

1. ____________________
2. ____________________
3. ____________________
4. ____________________
5. ____________________
6. ____________________
7. ____________________
8. ____________________
9. ____________________
10. ____________________
11. ____________________
12. ____________________

 Name________________________ Date______________

## ANSWERS TO SECTION 18.2 EXERCISES (text, p. 791)

### Exercise 1, p. 791

1. Gorry and Associates
Income Statement Data
19–2 to 19–5

| | Year 1 | Year 2 | Year 3 | Year 4 | Year 5 |
|---|---|---|---|---|---|
| Sales | | | | | |
| Cost of Goods Sold | | | | | |
| Gross Profit | | | | | |
| Operating Expenses | | | | | |
| Net Income | | | | | |

2. ____________________________________________
____________________________________________
____________________________________________

### Exercise 2, p. 791

1. Surrey Industries
Income Statement Data
19–1 to 19–5

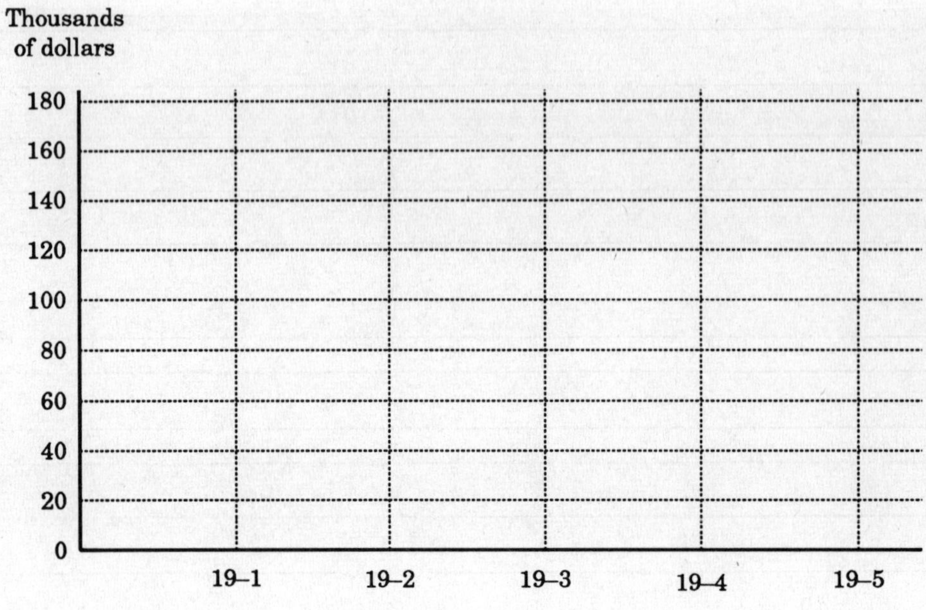


2. ____________________________________________
____________________________________________

## SECTION 18.2 EXERCISES (cont.)

**Exercise 3, p. 792**

**1.**

Goodenough Company

| | 19–1 | 19–2 | 19–3 | 19–4 | 19–5 |
|---|---|---|---|---|---|
| Current Assets | $50 000 | $55 000 | $59 500 | $64 000 | $68 500 |
| Current Liabilities | 35 000 | 38 000 | 40 000 | 42 500 | 45 000 |
| Working Capital | | | | | |

**2.**

Goodenough Company
Balance Sheet Data
19–1 to 19–5

| | 19–1 | 19–2 | 19–3 | 19–4 | 19–5 |
|---|---|---|---|---|---|
| Current Assets | | | | | |
| Current Liabilities | | | | | |
| Working Capital | | | | | |

## SECTION 18.2 EXERCISES (cont.)

**Ex. 3 (cont.)**

**3.**

Goodenough Company
Balance Sheet Data
19–1 to 19–5

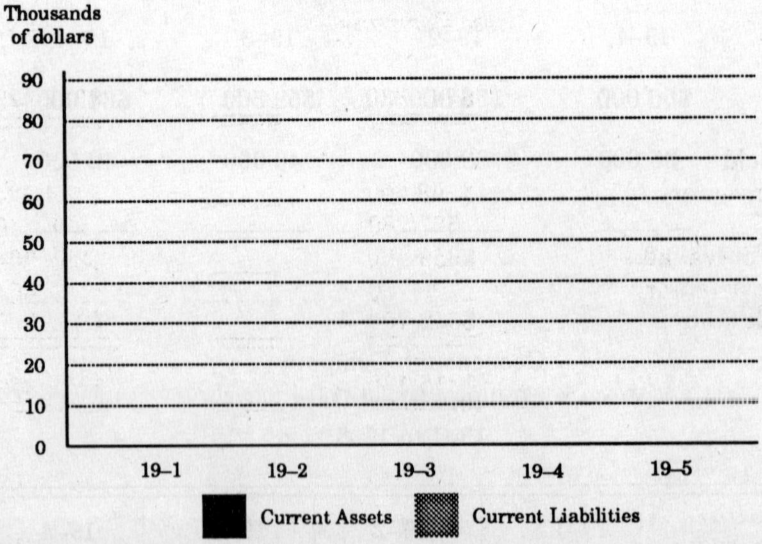


**Exercise 4, p. 792**

Comparative Balance Sheets
Rose Company and Lily Company
December 31, 19 – 6

| | *Rose Company* $ | % | *Lily Company* $ | % |
|---|---|---|---|---|
| ASSETS | | | | |
| Bank | $ 41 474 | ____ | $ 34 971 | ____ |
| Accounts Receivable | 44 371 | ____ | 24 008 | ____ |
| Merchandise Inventory | 106 780 | ____ | 42 464 | ____ |
| Plant & Equipment | 183 538 | ____ | 26 725 | ____ |
| Automobiles | 25 675 | ____ | 8 390 | ____ |
| Total Assets | $401 838 | ____ | $136 558 | ____ |
| LIABILITIES AND EQUITY | | | | |
| Accounts Payable | $ 86 480 | ____ | $ 13 940 | ____ |
| Bank Loan | 50 000 | ____ | | ____ |
| Mortgage Payable | 120 000 | ____ | ____ | ____ |
| Total Liabilities | $256 480 | ____ | $ 13 940 | ____ |
| Owner's Equity | | | | |
| Beginning Capital | $114 728 | ____ | $118 539 | ____ |
| Net Income | 105 630 | ____ | 29 079 | ____ |
| | $220 358 | ____ | $147 618 | ____ |
| Drawings | 75 000 | ____ | 25 000 | ____ |
| Ending Capital | $145 358 | ____ | $122 618 | ____ |
| Total Liabilities and Equity | $401 838 | ____ | $136 558 | ____ |

## SECTION 18.2 EXERCISES (cont.)

**Ex. 4 (cont.)**

Comparative Income Statements
Rose Company and Lily Company
December 31, 19 – 6

| | *Rose Company* $ | % | *Lily Company* $ | % |
|---|---|---|---|---|
| Sales | $767 830 | | $332 879 | |
| Cost of Goods Sold | | | | |
| Beginning Inventory | $ 98 200 | | $ 44 224 | |
| Purchases | 561 280 | | 208 740 | |
| Cost of Goods Available | $659 480 | | $252 964 | |
| Less Ending Inventory | 106 780 | | 42 464 | |
| Cost of Goods Sold | $552 700 | | $210 500 | |
| Gross Profit | $215 130 | | $122 379 | |
| Operating Expenses | | | | |
| Bank Interest | $ 7 000 | | $ 1 000 | |
| Mortgage Interest | 11 250 | | | |
| Depreciation Equipment | 5 500 | | 6 600 | |
| Depreciation Automobiles | 10 000 | | 3 500 | |
| Rent | | | 24 000 | |
| Wages | 35 750 | | 47 500 | |
| Other Expenses | 40 000 | | 10 700 | |
| Total Expenses | $109 500 | | $93 300 | |
| Net Income | $105 630 | | $29 079 | |

2. a. ____________________

b. ____________________

____________________

____________________

## SECTION 18.2 EXERCISES (cont.)

**Exercise 5, p. 793**

1.

PLAYFAIR COMPANY
COMPARATIVE BALANCE SHEET
DECEMBER 31, 19–4 AND 19–3

| | *19 – 4* | *19 – 3* | *Increase or Decrease (–)* | *% Change* |
|---|---|---|---|---|
| ASSETS | | | | |
| *Current Assets* | | | | |
| Bank | $ 9 090 | $ 5 500 | | |
| Accounts Receivable | 65 220 | 35 700 | | |
| Merchandise Inventory | 67 096 | 42 100 | | |
| Prepaid Expenses | 3 540 | 3 500 | | |
| Total Current Assets | $144 946 | $86 800 | | |
| *Fixed Assets* | | | | |
| Land | $ 50 000 | $ 50 000 | | |
| Buildings (Net) | 135 000 | 138 000 | | |
| Equipment (Net) | 141 000 | 160 000 | | |
| Automobiles (Net) | 25 000 | 30 000 | | |
| Total Fixed Assets | $351 000 | $378 000 | | |
| Total Assets | $495 946 | $464 800 | | |
| LIABILITIES AND OWNER'S EQUITY | | | | |
| *Current Liabilities* | | | | |
| Accounts Payable | $ 97 936 | $ 52 750 | | |
| Bank Loan | 50 000 | 50 000 | | |
| Total Current Liabilities | $147 936 | $102 750 | | |
| *Long-Term Liability* | | | | |
| Mortgage Payable | $ 70 000 | $ 75 000 | | |
| Total Liabilities | $217 936 | $177 750 | | |
| *T. Jennings, Capital* | | | | |
| Capital, January 1 | $287 050 | $277 700 | | |
| Net Income | 90 960 | 84 350 | | |
| | $378 010 | $362 050 | | |
| Drawings | 100 000 | 75 000 | | |
| Capital, December 31 | $278 010 | $287 050 | | |
| Total Liabilities & Equity | $495 946 | $464 800 | | |

## SECTION 18.2 EXERCISES (cont.)

**Ex. 5 (cont.)**

**2.** ______________________________

## ANSWERS TO SECTION 18.3 REVIEW QUESTIONS (text, p. 799)

### Simple Ratios and Percentages

1. a. ______________________________
   b. ______________________________
   c. ______________________________
   d. ______________________________
   e. ______________________________
   f. ______________________________
2. ______________________________
3. ______________________________
4. ______________________________
5. ______________________________

## ANSWERS TO SECTION 18.3 EXERCISES (text, p. 800)

### Exercise 1, p. 800 Schooner Company

| 1. Ratio or Percentage | | 2. Comment |
|---|---|---|
| Current ratio | ______ | ____________________ |
| Quick ratio | ______ | ____________________ |
| Debt ratio | ______ | ____________________ |
| Equity ratio | ______ | ____________________ |
| Return on net sales | ______ | ____________________ |
| Return on owner's equity | ______ | ____________________ |

### Exercise 2, p. 801 The Cloverdale Company

| 1. Ratio or Percentage | | 2. Comment |
|---|---|---|
| Current ratio | ______ | ____________________ |
| Quick ratio | ______ | ____________________ |
| Debt ratio | ______ | ____________________ |
| Equity ratio | ______ | ____________________ |
| Return on net sales | ______ | ____________________ |
| Return on owner's equity | ______ | ____________________ |

## SECTION 18.3 EXERCISES (cont.)

**Exercise 3, p. 803** **Company A, Company B**

1.

| | Ratio | Company A | Company B |
|---|---|---|---|
| a. | Current ratio | | |
| b. | Quick ratio | | |
| c. | Debt ratio | | |
| d. | Equity ratio | | |
| e. | Rate of return on net sales | | |
| f. | Rate of return on equity | | |

2.

## ANSWERS TO SECTION 18.4 REVIEW QUESTIONS (text, p. 807)
## Additional Ratios, Percentages, and Statistics

1.
2.
3.
4.
5.
6.
7.
8.
9.
10.

# Chapter 18

Name________________________ Date______________

## ANSWERS TO SECTION 18.4 EXERCISES (text, p. 808)

**Exercise 1, p. 808 Saturn Sales Company**

| Description | Ratio | Opinion |
|---|---|---|
| 1. Current ratio | | |
| 2. Quick ratio | | |
| 3. Collection period | | |
| 4. Inventory turnover | | |
| 5. Net income percentage | | |
| 6. Return on investment | | |
| 7. Debt ratio | | |
| 8. Equity ratio | | |
| 9. Times interest earned | | |

**Exercise 2, p. 809**

CALVINO COMPANY

INCOME STATEMENT

YEAR ENDED DECEMBER 31, 19–8

| | |
|---|---|
| *Revenue* | |
| Sales | $170 000 |
| *Cost of Goods Sold* | |
| Opening Inventory | |
| Purchases | $128 500 |
| Goods Available for Sale | |
| Closing Inventory | |
| Cost of Goods Sold | $129 000 |
| *Gross Profit* | $ |
| *Operating Expenses* | $ |
| *Net Income* | $ |

## ANSWERS TO SECTION 18.4 EXERCISES (cont.)

**Ex. 2 (cont.)**

CALVINO COMPANY
BALANCE SHEET
DECEMBER 31, 19 – 8

| | |
|---|---|
| ASSETS | |
| *Current Assets* | |
| Bank | $ 3 700 |
| Accounts Receivable | |
| Merchandise Inventory | 10 500 |
| Total Current Assets | $ |
| *Plant and Equipment* | |
| Land | $ 35 000 |
| Buildings and Equipment | |
| Total Plant and Equipment | $ |
| Total Assets | $ |
| LIABILITIES AND OWNER'S EQUITY | |
| *Current Liabilities* | |
| Bank Loan | $ 15 000 |
| Accounts Payable | |
| Total Current Liabilities | $ |
| *Owner's Equity* | |
| Beginning Capital | $ 134 750 |
| Add: Net Income | |
| Deduct: Drawings | $ |
| Ending Capital | $ |
| Total Liabilities and Owner's Equity | $ |

## ANSWERS TO SECTION 18.4 EXERCISES (cont.)

**Exercise 3, p. 811 Pluto Company and Neptune Company**

| KEY RATIOS AND STATISTICS | | |
|---|---|---|
| *Description* | *Pluto* | *Neptune* |
| Current ratio | | |
| Quick ratio | | |
| Collection period | | |
| Inventory turnover | | |
| Net income percentage | | |
| Return on investment | | |
| Debt ratio | | |
| Equity ratio | | |
| Times interest earned | | |

**2.** ____________________

____________________

____________________

**3.** ____________________

## ANSWERS TO SECTION 18.4 EXERCISES (cont.)

### Exercise 4, p. 812

1. For each of the following situations work out the earnings per share figure and the price earnings ratio to one decimal place.

| *Corporation* | *A* | *B* | *C* | *D* |
|---|---|---|---|---|
| Net income for year | $172 647 | $2 350 700 | $85 362 | $312 062 |
| Number of shares | 100 000 | 1 200 000 | 10 000 | 500 000 |
| Market value per share | $32.50 | $23.50 | $125 | $5 |
| Earnings per share | | | | |
| Price-earnings ratio | | | | |
| *Corporation* | *E* | *F* | *G* | *H* |
| Net income for year | $1 250 000 | $257 680 | $102 000 | $569 251 |
| Number of shares | 126 500 | 350 000 | 250 000 | 100 000 |
| Market value per share | $100 | $18 | $8 | $50 |
| Earnings per share | | | | |
| Price-earnings ratio | | | | |

2. On the basis of your calculations, which company's shares appear to be the best buy?

### Exercise 5, p. 813

| | a | b | c | d | e |
|---|---|---|---|---|---|
| No. of shares | 50 000 | 120 000 | | | 8 000 |
| Net income | $130 000 | $180 000 | $125 000 | $75 0000 | $72 0000 |
| Earnings per share | | | $5.00 | $2.50 | $9.00 |
| Market value | $52 | $18 | | | $45 |
| Price-earnings ratio | | | 8 | 16 | |

# Chapter 18

Name______________________ Date______________

## ANSWERS TO COMPUTER REVIEW 18.5 QUESTIONS (text, p. 819)

1. ______________________________

2. ______________________________

## COMMUNICATE IT (text, p. 819)

______________________________

## ANSWERS TO CHAPTER 18 EXERCISES (text, p. 820)

### USING YOUR KNOWLEDGE

**Exercise 1, p. 820**

1. The condensed financial statements of Magnus Company for the years 19–5 and 19–6 are shown below.
   1. Complete the Net Change column of the comparative balance sheet.
   2. Complete the Per Cent columns of the comparative income statement.

MAGNUS COMPANY
COMPARATIVE BALANCE SHEET
DECEMBER 31, 19 – 5 AND 19 – 6

| | *19 – 5* | *19 – 6* | *Net Change* |
|---|---|---|---|
| ASSETS | | | |
| Bank | $ 13 000 | $ 960 | $ |
| Accounts Receivable | 29 500 | 35 200 | |
| Merchandise Inventory | 37 450 | 38 950 | |
| Prepaid Expenses | 3 700 | 2 600 | |
| Land | 64 500 | 64 500 | |
| Buildings | 90 000 | 166 500 | |
| Equipment | 75 000 | 146 400 | |
| Automobiles | 30 000 | 21 000 | |
| | $ 343 150 | $ 476 110 | $ |
| LIABILITIES AND EQUITY | | | |
| Bank Loan | $ 40 000 | $ 200 000 | $ |
| Accounts Payable | 26 500 | 18 700 | |
| Mortgage Payable | 125 300 | 112 770 | |
| Owner's Equity | 151 350 | 144 640 | |
| | $ 343 150 | $ 476 110 | $ |

## ANSWERS TO CHAPTER 18 EXERCISES (cont.)

**Ex. 1 (cont.)**

**2.**

MAGNUS COMPANY
COMPARATIVE INCOME STATEMENT
YEARS ENDED DECEMBER 31, 19 – 5 AND 19 – 6

| | *19 – 5* Amount | *19 – 5* Per Cent | *19 – 6* Amount | *19 – 6* Per Cent |
|---|---|---|---|---|
| *Sales* | $ 289 500 | | $ 309 120 | |
| *Cost of Goods Sold* | 142 750 | | 155 700 | |
| *Gross Profit* | $ 146 750 | | $ 153 420 | |
| *Operating Expenses* | | | | |
| Advertising | $ 1 500 | | $ 1 500 | |
| Car Expenses | 4 000 | | 4 050 | |
| Depreciation of Building | 4 250 | | 8 500 | |
| Depreciation of Equipment | 18 000 | | 29 280 | |
| Depreciation of Automobiles | 9 000 | | 9 000 | |
| Power | 3 500 | | 3 950 | |
| Interest and Bank Charges | 16 530 | | 36 530 | |
| Supplies Used | 1 000 | | 1 100 | |
| Wages | 36 700 | | 38 900 | |
| Total Operating Expenses | $ 94 480 | | $ 132 810 | |
| *Net Income* | $ 52 270 | | $ 20 610 | |

**3.** **a.** ______________________________

**b.** ______________________________

**c.** ______________________________

**d.** ______________________________

**4.** ______________________________

**5.** ______________________________

## ANSWERS TO CHAPTER 18 EXERCISES (cont.)

**Exercise 2, p. 822**

**On p. 822 of your text and p. 269 of your Workbook is the partially completed common-size comparative statement for two companies in the same line of business. You are preparing this analysis with a view to making an investment in one of the two companies.**

1. **Complete the common-size income statement on p. 269 of the Workbook. (Calculations to one decimal place.)**
2. Answer the following questions.
   a. Which company has the larger net income?
   b. Which company has the larger percentage net income?
   c. Which company has the larger investment in inventory?
   d. Which company has the larger gross income percentage?
   e. Which company does not own its own building?
   f. What are the three clues to question e?
   g. If the owners' average equities are $80 000 for Company A, and $30 000 for Company B, calculate the respective returns on owners' investment.
   h. Which company gives the greater return on owners' investment?
   i. Which company has the greater interest-bearing debt?
   j. How much is Company B disadvantaged by not owning its own building?
   k. Listed below are factors that favour Company A or Company B. For each one, indicate the company favoured on p. 270 of the Workbook.
      i. greater net income
      ii. higher gross income percentage
      iii. greater return on owners' investment
      iv. more established, owns own building
      v. lower inventory
      vi. lower expense
      vii. greater potential to reduce expenses
      viii. greater share of market (sales)
      ix. fewer interest-bearing debts.
   l. In which company would you choose to invest? Give reasons.

## ANSWERS TO CHAPTER 18 EXERCISES (cont.)

**Ex.2 (cont.)**

**1. (cont.)**

COMMON-SIZE COMPARATIVE INCOME STATEMENT
YEAR ENDED DECEMBER 31, 19 – 3

| | *Dollars* | | *Percentage of Sales* | |
|---|---|---|---|---|
| | Co. A | Co. B | Co. A | Co. B |
| *Sales* | $ 200 000 | $150 000 | | |
| *Cost of Goods Sold* | | | | |
| Opening Inventory | $ 50 000 | $ 25 000 | | |
| Purchases | 123 000 | 81 200 | | |
| Goods Available for Sale | $ 173 000 | $106 200 | | |
| Less Closing Inventory | 57 000 | 24 000 | | |
| Cost of Goods Sold | $ 116 000 | $ 82 200 | | |
| *Gross Profit* | $ 84 000 | $ 67 800 | | |
| *Operating Expenses* | | | | |
| Advertising | $ 5 000 | $ 4 000 | | |
| Bank Interest | 900 | 10 000 | | |
| Depreciation Building | 10 000 | — | | |
| Depreciation Equipment | 4 500 | 3 000 | | |
| General Expense | 1 900 | 1 500 | | |
| Insurance | 500 | 400 | | |
| Postage | 750 | 350 | | |
| Property Tax | 2 000 | — | | |
| Rent | — | 18 000 | | |
| Telephone | 450 | 300 | | |
| Wages | 13 740 | 9 500 | | |
| Total Expenses | $ 39 740 | $ 47 050 | | |
| *Net Income* | $ 44 260 | $ 20 750 | | |

**2.** **a.** ______________ **f.** ______________

**b.** ______________ **g.** ______________

**c.** ______________ **h.** ______________

**d.** ______________ **i.** ______________

**e.** ______________ **j.** ______________

## ANSWERS TO CHAPTER 18 EXERCISES (cont.)

**Ex.2 (cont.)**

**2. (cont.)**

**k.**

| | | Favours Co.A | Favours Co. B |
|---|---|---|---|
| i. | Greater net income. | | |
| ii. | Higher gross income percentage. | | |
| iii. | Greater return on owners' investment. | | |
| iv. | More established, owns own building. | | |
| v. | Lower inventory. | | |
| vi. | Lower expense. | | |
| vii. | Greater potential to reduce expenses. | | |
| viii. | Greater share of market (sales). | | |
| ix. | Fewer interest-bearing debts. | | |

**l.** Both companies seem to be financially healthy. Company B is handicapped slightly by not owning its own building.

A firm decision regarding which company to invest in is not possible without knowing the asking prices. If the asking price for both companies is approximately the same, then Company A is favoured. But if there is a significant difference in the two asking prices, say twice as much for Company A, then Company B might be a better choice.

**Exercise 3, p. 823**

SPARTA COMPANY
INCOME STATEMENT
YEAR ENDED DECEMBER 31, 19–3

| | |
|---|---|
| Sales | $ |
| Cost of Goods Sold | |
| Beginning Inventory | $ |
| Purchases | |
| Goods Available for Sale | $ |
| Less Ending Inventory | 21 000 |
| Cost of Goods Sold | $ 170 000 |
| Gross Profit | $ |
| Operating Expenses | $ 114 375 |
| Net Income | $ |

## ANSWERS TO CHAPTER 18 EXERCISES (cont.)

**Ex.3 (cont.)**

SPARTA COMPANY
BALANCE SHEET
DECEMBER 31, 19 – 3

| ASSETS | |
|---|---|
| Current Assets | |
| Bank | $ |
| Accounts Receivable | 35 000 |
| Merchandise Inventory | 21 000 |
| Total Current Assets | $ |
| Fixed Assets | |
| Land | $ 50 000 |
| Plant and Equipment | |
| Total Fixed Assets | $ 120 000 |
| Total Assets | $ |
| LIABILITIES AND EQUITY | |
| Current Liabilities | |
| Accounts Payable | $ |
| Bank Loan | 20 000 |
| Total Current Liabilities | $ 32 000 |
| Owner's Equity | |
| Beginning Capital | $ 130 000 |
| Net Income | |
| | $ |
| Drawings | |
| Ending Capital | $ |
| Total Liabilities and Equity | $ |

## ANSWERS TO CHAPTER 18 EXERCISES (cont.)

### COMPREHENSIVE EXERCISES

**Exercise 4, p. 825**

**1.**

ANSON COMPANY
COMPARATIVE BALANCE SHEET
YEARS ENDED DECEMBER 31, 19 – 7 AND 19 – 8

| | *19 – 7* | *19 – 8* | *Net Change* |
|---|---|---|---|
| ASSETS | | | |
| *Current Assets* | | | |
| Bank | $ 4 000 | $ 509 000 | $ |
| Merchandise Inventory | 50 000 | 50 000 | |
| | $ 54 000 | $ 559 000 | $ |
| *Fixed Assets* | | | |
| Land | $ 380 000 | $ 80 000 | $ |
| Buildings | 80 000 | 76 000 | |
| Equipment | 90 000 | 72 000 | |
| | $ 550 000 | $ 228 000 | $ |
| Total Assets | $ 604 000 | $ 787 000 | $ |
| LIABILITIES AND EQUITY | | | |
| *Current Liabilities* | | | |
| Bank Loan | $ 20 000 | — | $ |
| Accounts Payable | 42 000 | $ 12 000 | |
| | $ 62 000 | $ 12 000 | $ |
| *Owner's Equity* | | | |
| R. Anson, Capital | $ 542 000 | $ 775 000 | $ |
| Total Liabilities and Equity | $ 604 000 | $ 787 000 | $ |

**2.** a.

b.

c.

d.

e.

f.

## ANSWERS TO CHAPTER 18 EXERCISES (cont.)

**Ex. 4 (cont.)**

**g. Challenge**

Increases 1. ______________________

2. ______________________

Total Increases ________

Decreases 1. ______________________

2. ______________________

3. ______________________

Total Decreases ________

Net Increase $505 000

**Exercise 5, p. 827**

**Exercise 6, p. 827**

 Name ______________________ Date ________________

## ANSWERS TO CHAPTER 18 EXERCISES (cont.)

**Exercise 7, p. 828**

1. ______
2. ______
3. ______
4. ______
5. ______

## FOR FURTHER THOUGHT

**Exercise 8, p. 828**

1. ______
2. ______
3. ______
4. ______
5. ______
6. ______
7. ______

## ANSWERS TO CHAPTER 18 EXERCISES (cont.)

**Ex. 8 (cont.)**

**8.**

**9.**

**10.**

**11.**

a.

b.

**12.**

**13.**

a.

b.

c.

d.

e.

**14.**

**15.**

 Name________________________ Date__________

## CASE STUDIES (text, p. 829)

**Case 1** *Owning Your Own Business: A Blessing or a Curse?*, p. 829

**1.**

| *Key Ratios and Statistics* | | |
|---|---|---|
| Description | 19–4 | 19–5 |
| Working Capital | | |
| Current Ratio | | |
| Quick Ratio | | |
| Collection Period | | |
| Inventory Turnover | | |
| Debt Ratio | | |
| Equity Ratio | | |
| Times Interest Earned | | |
| Rate of Return on Net Sales | | |
| Rate of Return on Equity | | |

## CASE STUDIES (cont.)

**Case 1 (cont.)**

**2. a.**

OZOLINS MEN'S WEAR
BALANCE SHEET
DECEMBER 31, 19 – 6

| | *19 – 6* | *19 – 5* | *Increase Decrease* |
|---|---|---|---|
| ASSETS | | | |
| *Current Assets* | | | |
| Bank | | | |
| Accounts Receivable | | | |
| Inventory | | | |
| Supplies | | | |
| Total Current Assets | | | |
| *Fixed Assets* | | | |
| Store Equipment | | | |
| Total Assets | | | |
| LIABILITIES AND EQUITY | | | |
| *Current Liabilities* | | | |
| Accounts Payable | | | |
| Bank Loan | | | |
| Total Current Liabilities | | | |
| *Owner's Equity* | | | |
| Beginning Capital | | | |
| Net Income | | | |
| | | | |
| Drawings | | | |
| Ending Capital | | | |
| Total Liabilities and Equity | | | |

## CASE STUDIES (cont.)

**Case 1 (cont.)**

**2. a. (cont.)**

OZOLINS MEN'S WEAR
INCOME STATEMENT
YEAR ENDED DECEMBER 31, 19 – 6

| | *19 – 6* | *19 – 5* | *Increase Decrease* |
|---|---|---|---|
| *Revenue* | | | |
| Sales | | | |
| *Cost of Goods Sold* | | | |
| Beginning Inventory | | | |
| Purchases and Freight | | | |
| Cost of Goods Available | | | |
| Less Closing Inventory | | | |
| | | | |
| Gross Profit | | | |
| *Operating Expenses* | | | |
| Advertising | | | |
| Bad Debts | | | |
| Depreciation Equipment | | | |
| Interest | | | |
| Miscellaneous | | | |
| Rent ($5 000 + 1% of Sales) | | | |
| Utilities | | | |
| Wages | | | |
| Total Expenses | | | |
| Net Income | | | |

## CASE STUDIES (cont.)

**Case 1 (cont.)**

**2. (cont.)**

**b.**

| *Key Ratios and Statistics* | |
|---|---|
| Description | Ratio |
| Working Capital | |
| Current Ratio | |
| Quick Ratio | |
| Collection Period | |
| Inventory Turnover | |
| Debt Ratio | |
| Equity Ratio | |
| Times Interest Earned | |
| Rate of Return on Net Sales | |
| Rate of Return on Equity | |

**3.**

**4.**

## CASE STUDIES (cont.)

**Case 2** *Is the Manager Competent?*, p. 833

**1.**

HANNA IMPORTING
INCOME STATEMENT
YEARS 19 – 1 AND 19 – 2

| | *19 – 1 (Hanna)* | *19 – 2 (Ans)* | *Net Change* |
|---|---|---|---|
| *Sales* | $315 000 | $ 480 000 | |
| *Cost of Goods Sold* | | | |
| Opening Inventory | $ 80 000 | $ 85 000 | |
| Purchases | 195 000 | 285 000 | |
| Goods Available for Sale | $275 000 | $ 370 000 | |
| Less Ending Inventory | 85 000 | 55 000 | |
| Cost of Goods Sold | $190 000 | $ 315 000 | |
| Gross Profit | $125 000 | $ 165 000 | |
| *Operating Expenses* | | | |
| Advertising | $ 2 000 | $ 7 000 | |
| Bad Debts | 300 | 2 500 | |
| Bank Interest | 10 000 | 5 000 | |
| Car Expense | 3 000 | 3 100 | |
| Depreciation of Car | 1 500 | 1 500 | |
| Delivery Expense | 9 000 | 8 000 | |
| Depreciation of Delivery Truck | 3 600 | — | |
| Light and Heat | 1 700 | 2 000 | |
| Miscellaneous Expense | 300 | 350 | |
| Rent | 13 000 | 16 500 | |
| Telephone | 400 | 500 | |
| Wages and Salaries | 24 500 | 55 000 | |
| Loss on Sale of Truck | | 2 000 | |
| Total Expenses | $ 69 300 | $ 103 450 | |
| Net Income | $ 55 700 | $ 61 550 | |

**2.** ______________________________________________

**3.** ______________________________________________

## CASE STUDIES (cont.)

**Case 2 (cont.)**

**4.** ______________

1. ______________
2. ______________
3. ______________
4. ______________
5. ______________
6. ______________
7. ______________

**5.** ______________

**Case 3** *To Lend or Not To Lend*, p. 835

**1.**

| *Key Ratios and Statistics* | *19–6* | *19–7* | *19–8* |
|---|---|---|---|
| Working Capital | | | |
| Current Ratio | | | |
| Quick Ratio | | | |
| Collection Period | | | |
| Inventory Turnover | | | |
| Debt Ratio | | | |
| Equity Ratio | | | |
| Times Interest Earned Ratio | | | |
| Rate of Return on Net Sales | | | |
| Rate of Return on Owner's Equity | | | |

**2.** ______________

Name ______________________ Date ______________

## CASE STUDIES (cont.)

### Case 3 (cont.)

**3.**

Estimated Income Statement
19–9 Fiscal Year

**4. Challenge**

Estimated Balance Sheet
19-9 Fiscal Year

## CASE STUDIES (cont.)

### Case 3 (cont.)

5. **Challenge**

 Name________________________ Date__________________

**ENTREPRENEUR** **Steven Syme/ Designer and Builder of Custom Homes**

**ANSWERS TO DISCUSSION QUESTIONS (text, p. 840)**

**1.** ____________________________________________

**2.** ____________________________________________

____________________________________________

**3.** ____________________________________________

**4.** ____________________________________________

____________________________________________

**5.** ____________________________________________

**6.** ____________________________________________

**7.** ____________________________________________